THE COLLECTED
ALISON DARE™

8.95

LITTLE MISS ADVENTURES

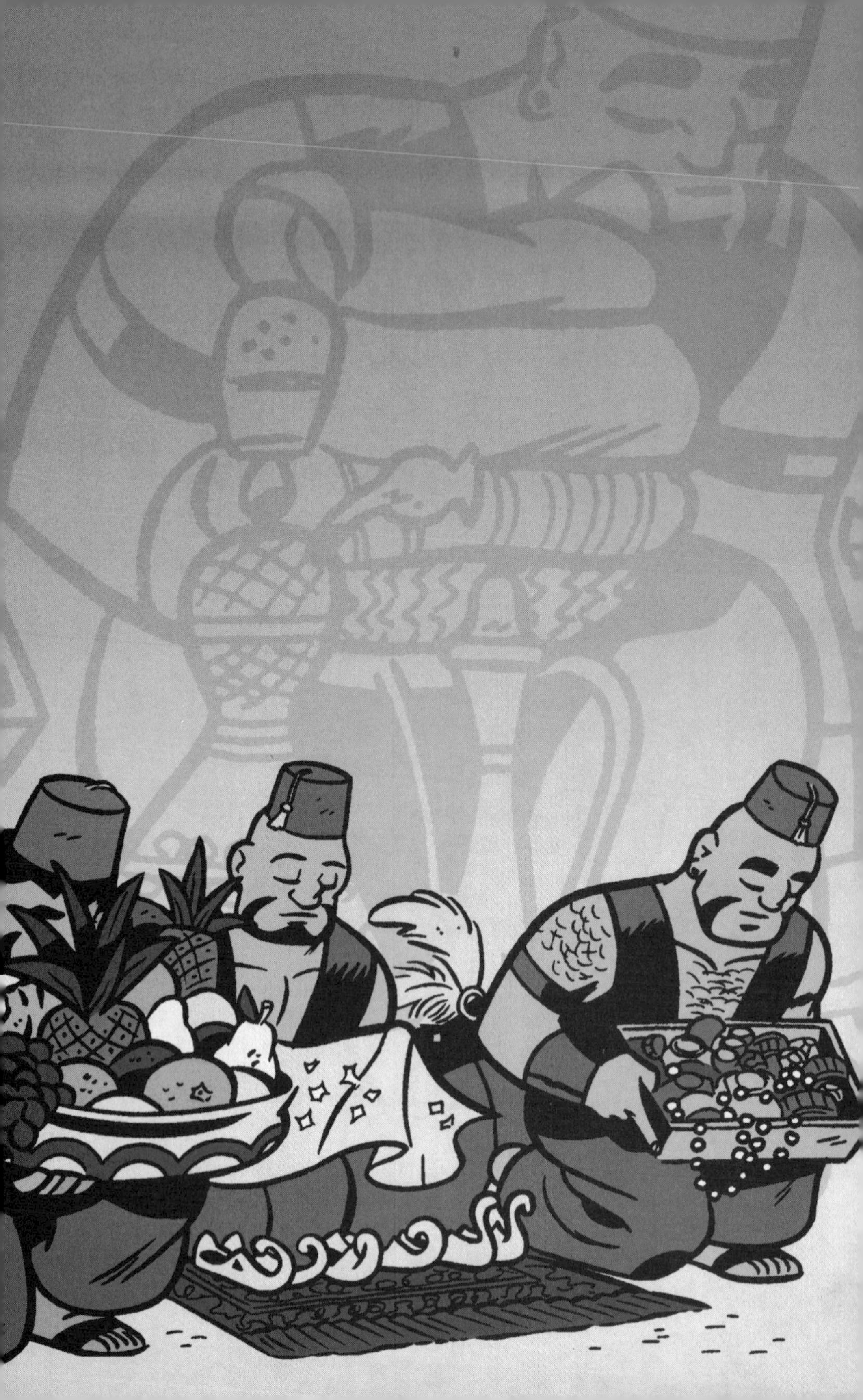

THE COLLECTED ALISON DARE
LITTLE MISS ADVENTURES

written by
J. Torres

illustrated by
J. Bone

book design by Kalah Allen

edited by James Lucas Jones

Graphic Marol
J Y

Published by Oni Press, Inc.

Joe Nozemack, publisher
Jamie S. Rich, editor in chief

This collects issues 1-3 of the Oni Press comics
series *The Return of Alison Dare,
Little Miss Adventures.*

ONI PRESS, INC.
6336 SE Milwaukie Avenue, PMB 30
Portland, OR 97202
USA

www.onipress.com

First edition: Febuary 2002
ISBN 1-929998-20-1

1 3 5 7 9 10 8 6 4 2
PRINTED IN CANADA.

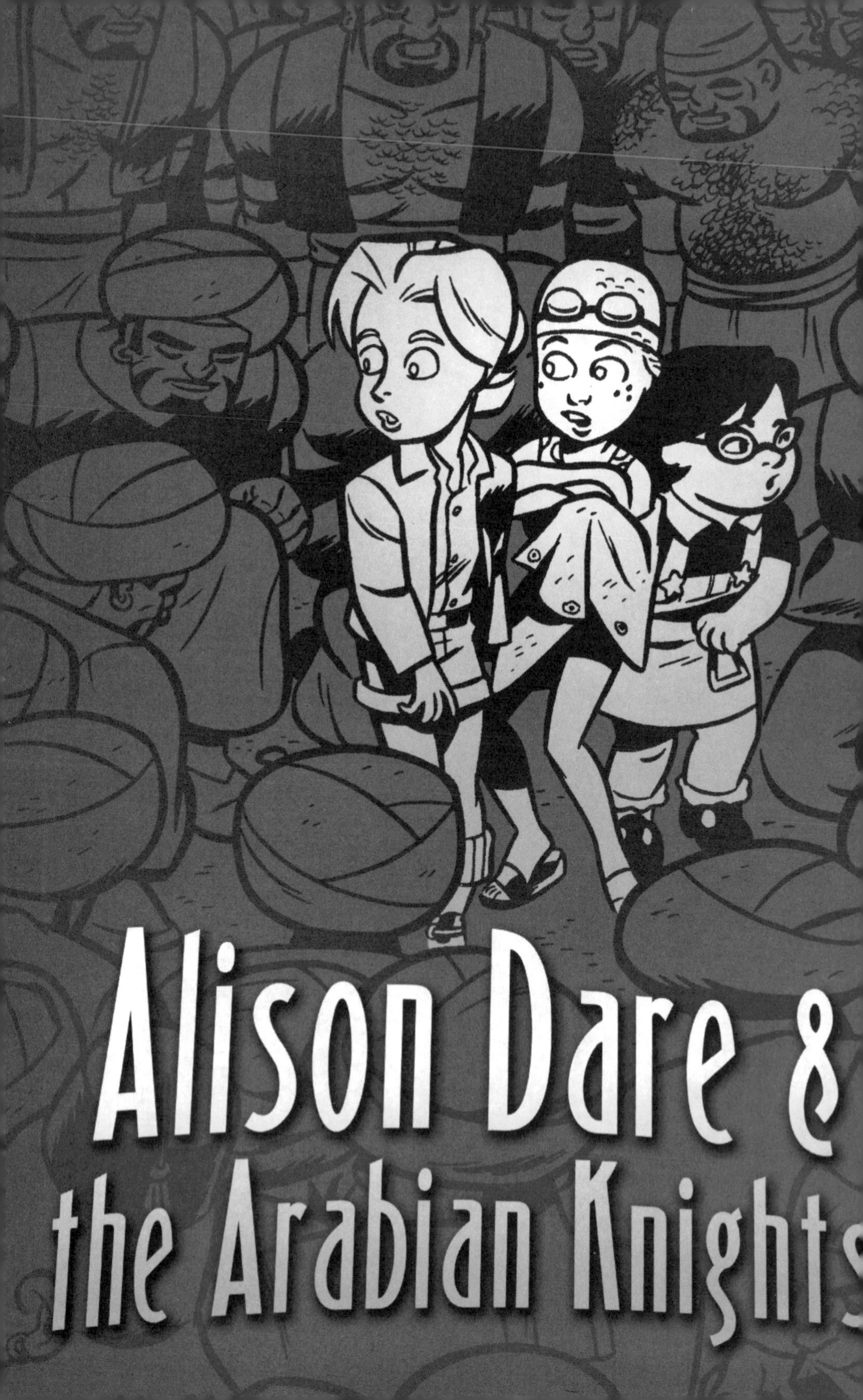
Alison Dare &
the Arabian Knights

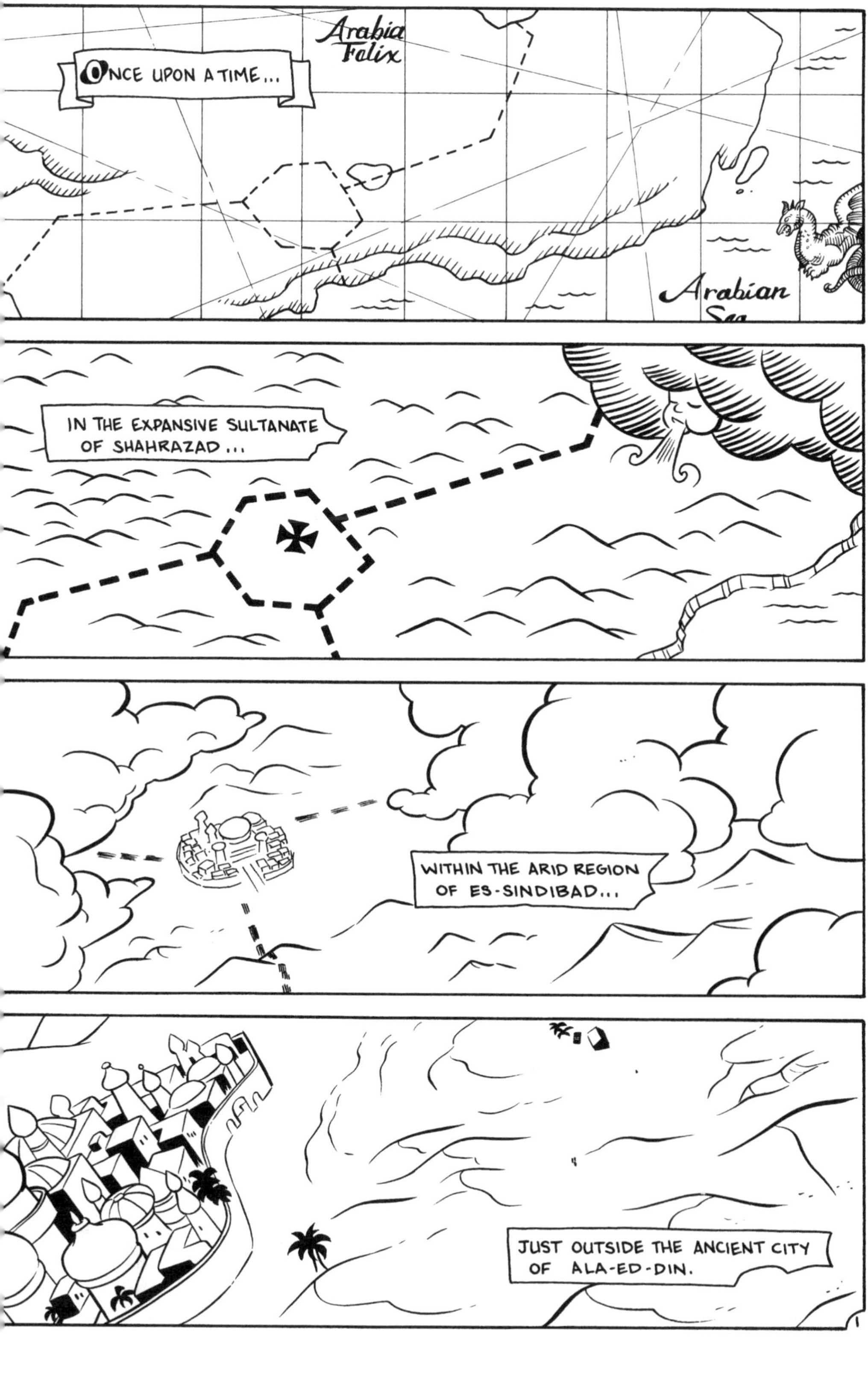
Arabia Felix
ONCE UPON A TIME...
Arabian
IN THE EXPANSIVE SULTANATE OF SHAHRAZAD...
WITHIN THE ARID REGION OF ES-SINDIBAD...
JUST OUTSIDE THE ANCIENT CITY OF ALA-ED-DIN.

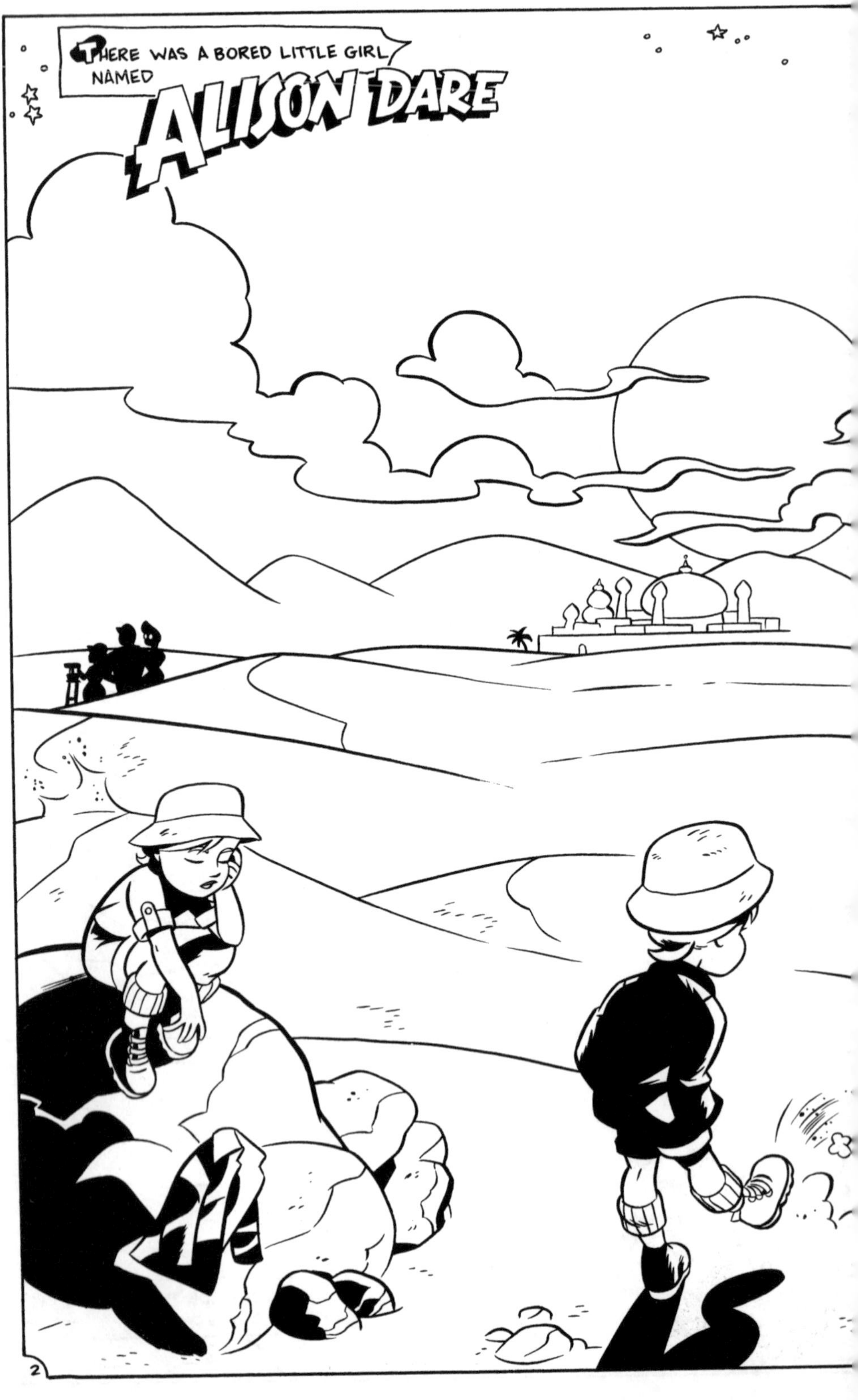
THERE WAS A BORED LITTLE GIRL NAMED
ALISON DARE

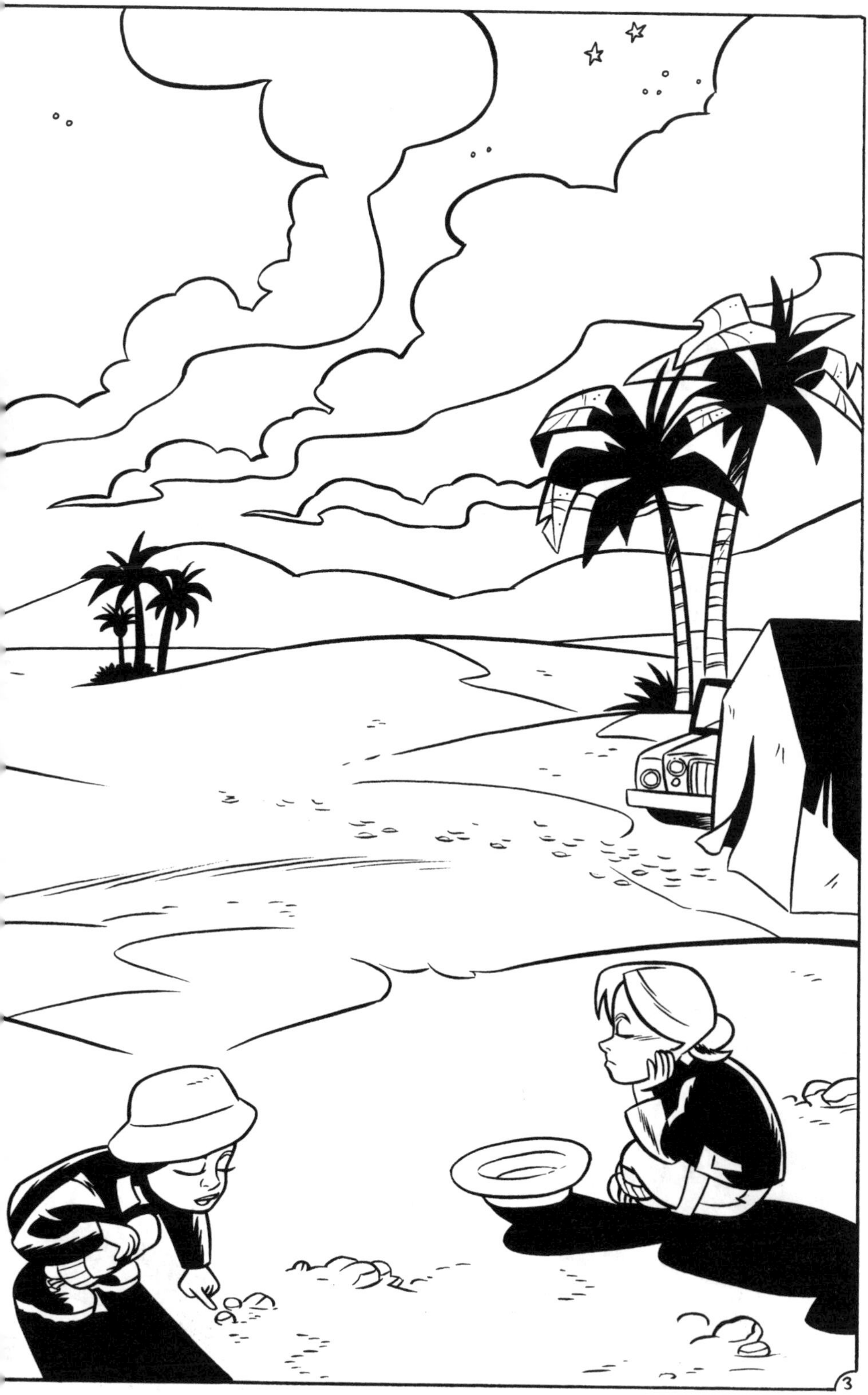

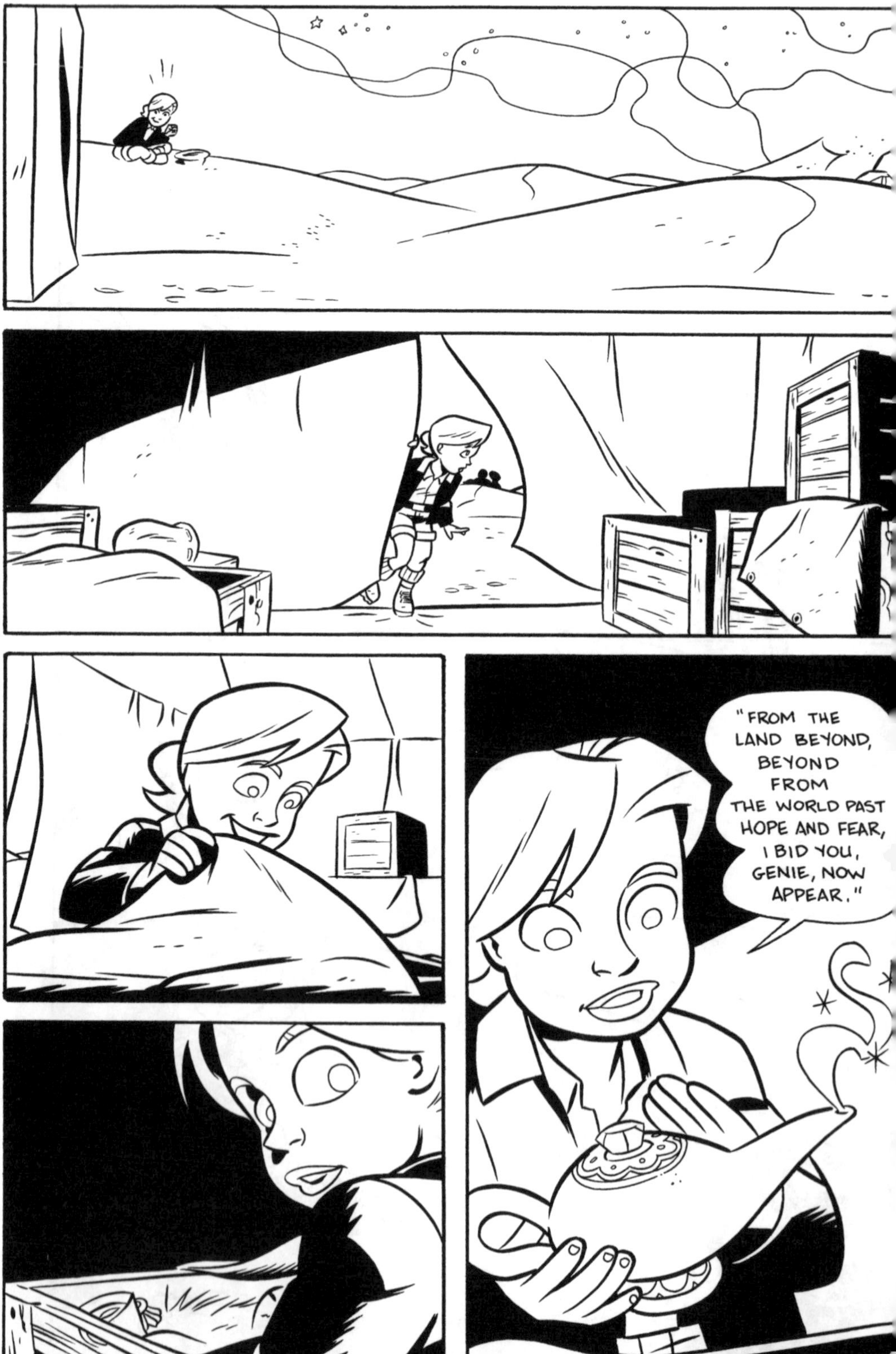
"FROM THE LAND BEYOND, BEYOND FROM THE WORLD PAST HOPE AND FEAR, I BID YOU, GENIE, NOW APPEAR."

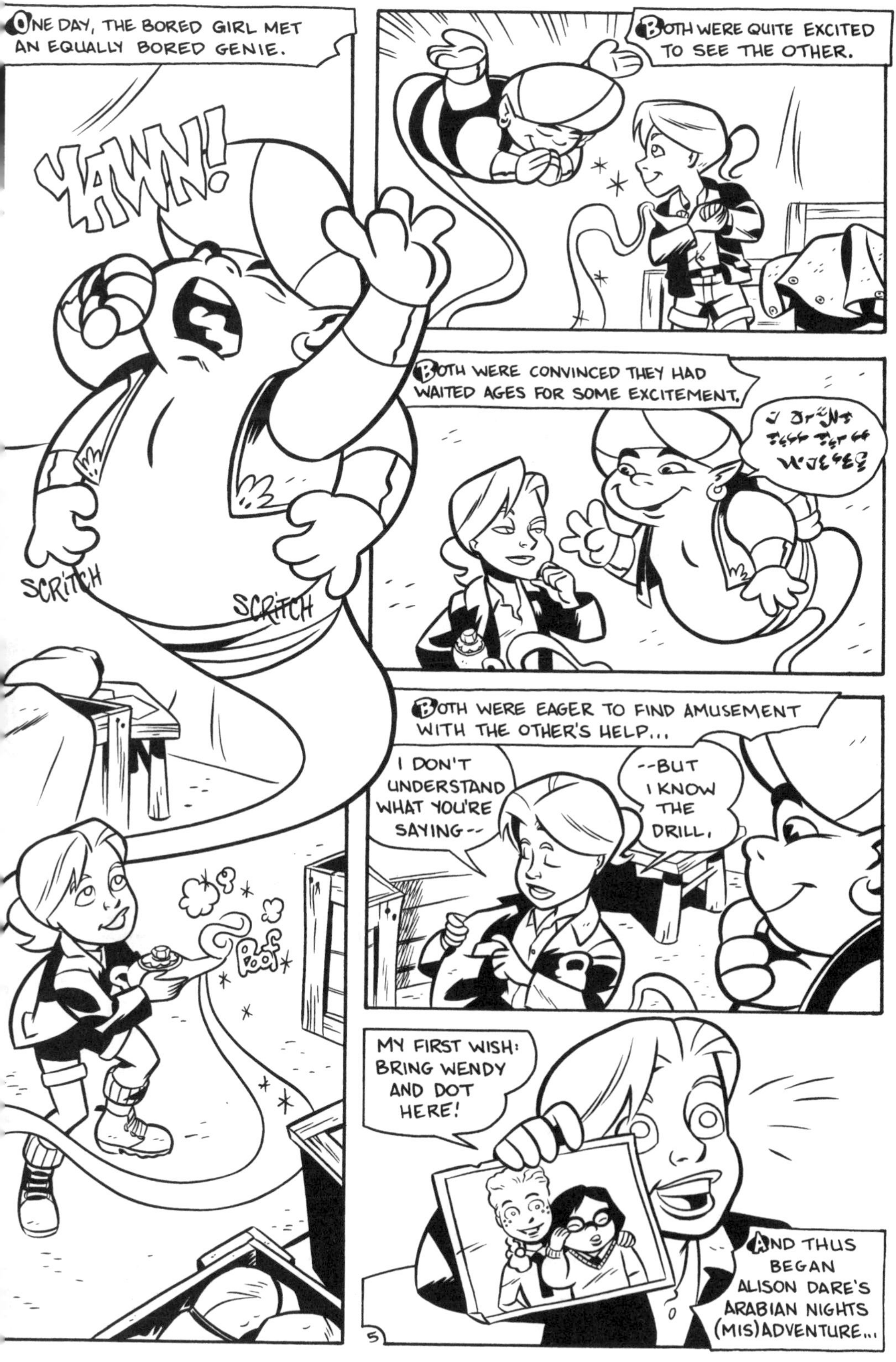
ONE DAY, THE BORED GIRL MET AN EQUALLY BORED GENIE.
YAWN!
SCRITCH
SCRITCH
POOF
BOTH WERE QUITE EXCITED TO SEE THE OTHER.
BOTH WERE CONVINCED THEY HAD WAITED AGES FOR SOME EXCITEMENT.
BOTH WERE EAGER TO FIND AMUSEMENT WITH THE OTHER'S HELP...
I DON'T UNDERSTAND WHAT YOU'RE SAYING--
--BUT I KNOW THE DRILL.
MY FIRST WISH: BRING WENDY AND DOT HERE!
AND THUS BEGAN ALISON DARE'S ARABIAN NIGHTS (MIS)ADVENTURE...

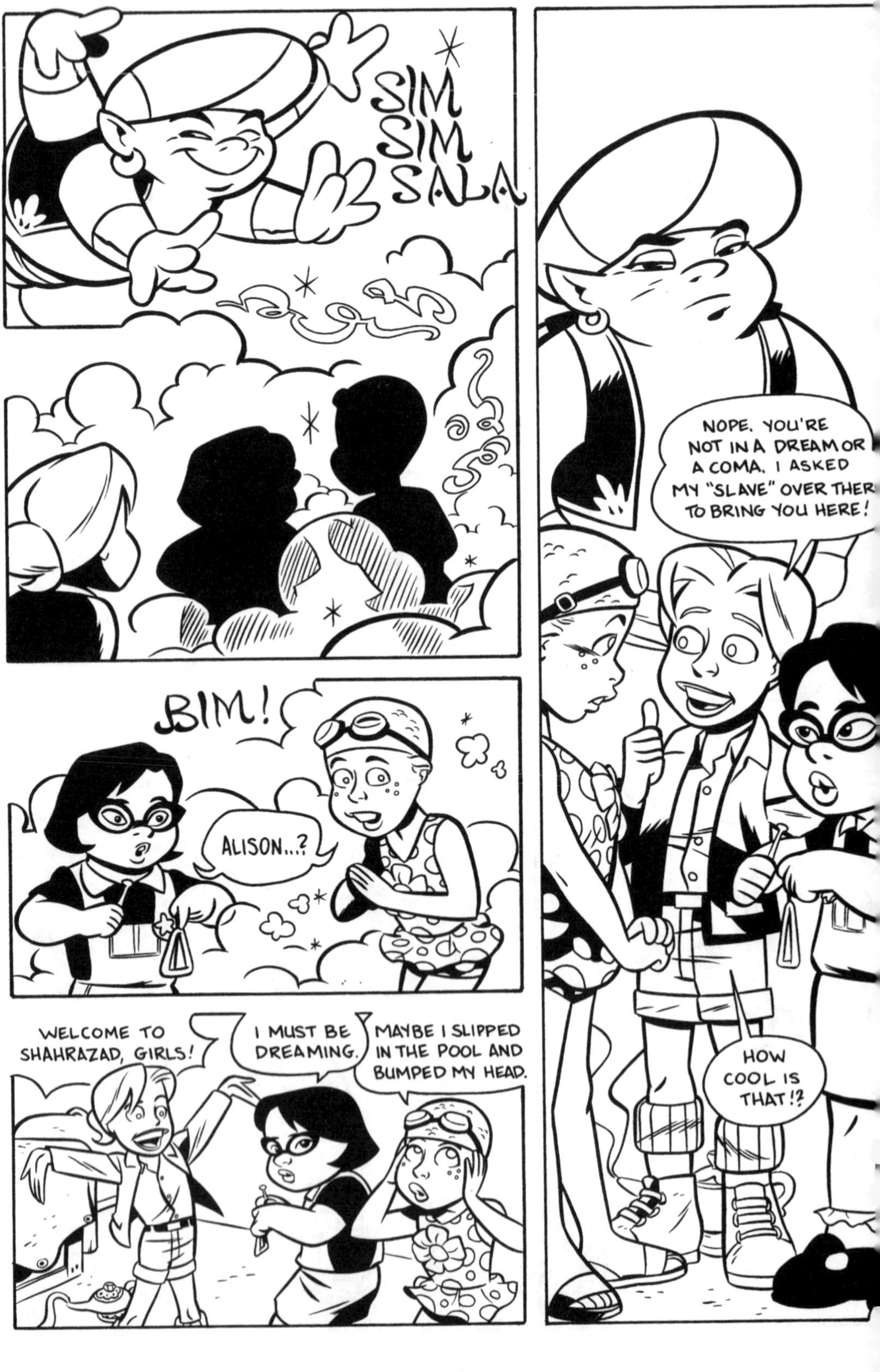
SIM SIM SALA
BIM!
ALISON...?
WELCOME TO SHAHRAZAD, GIRLS!
I MUST BE DREAMING.
MAYBE I SLIPPED IN THE POOL AND BUMPED MY HEAD.
NOPE. YOU'RE NOT IN A DREAM OR A COMA. I ASKED MY "SLAVE" OVER THER TO BRING YOU HERE!
HOW COOL IS THAT!?

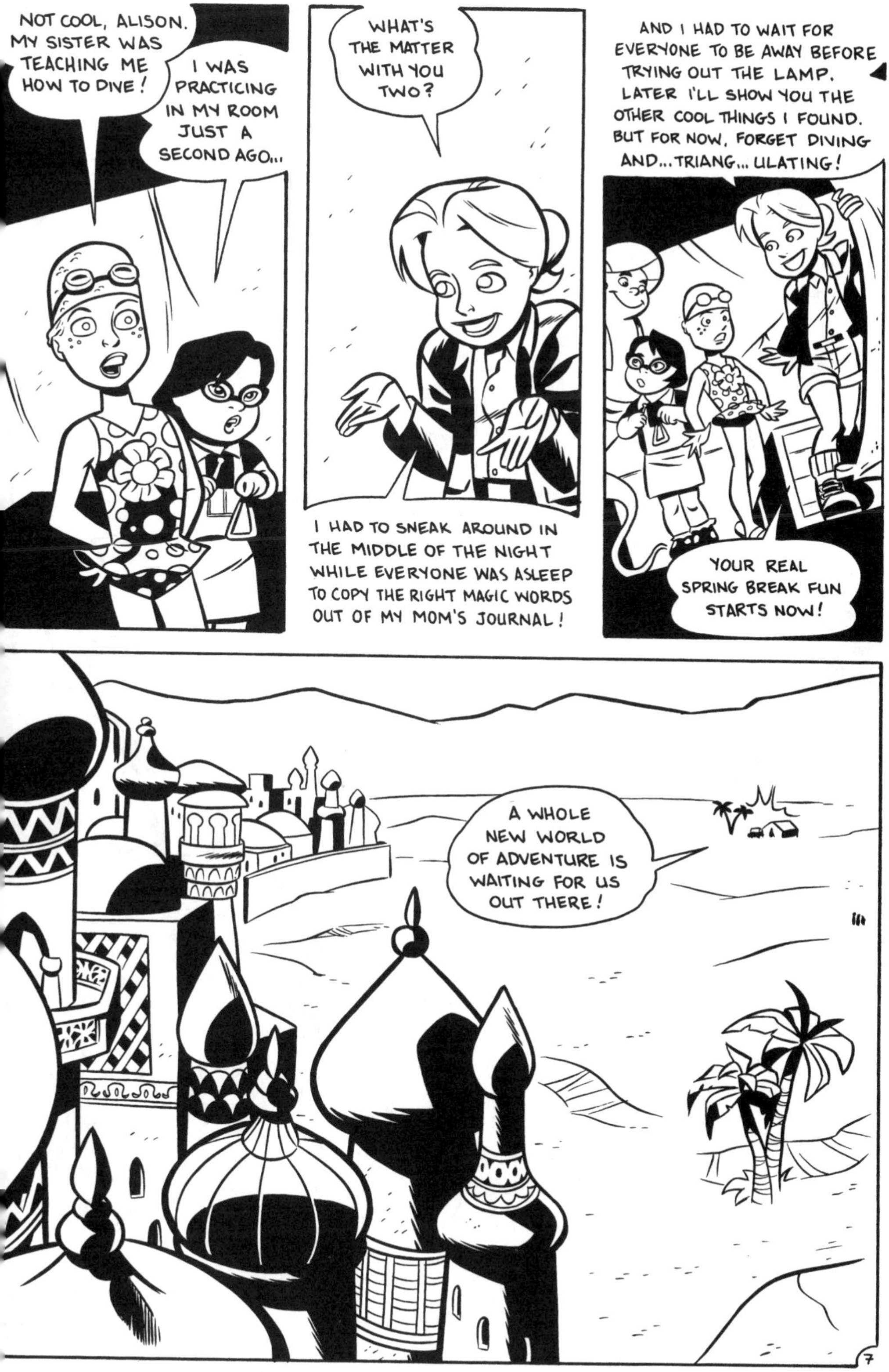
NOT COOL, ALISON. MY SISTER WAS TEACHING ME HOW TO DIVE!
I WAS PRACTICING IN MY ROOM JUST A SECOND AGO...
WHAT'S THE MATTER WITH YOU TWO?
I HAD TO SNEAK AROUND IN THE MIDDLE OF THE NIGHT WHILE EVERYONE WAS ASLEEP TO COPY THE RIGHT MAGIC WORDS OUT OF MY MOM'S JOURNAL!
AND I HAD TO WAIT FOR EVERYONE TO BE AWAY BEFORE TRYING OUT THE LAMP. LATER I'LL SHOW YOU THE OTHER COOL THINGS I FOUND. BUT FOR NOW, FORGET DIVING AND... TRIANG... ULATING!
YOUR REAL SPRING BREAK FUN STARTS NOW!
A WHOLE NEW WORLD OF ADVENTURE IS WAITING FOR US OUT THERE!

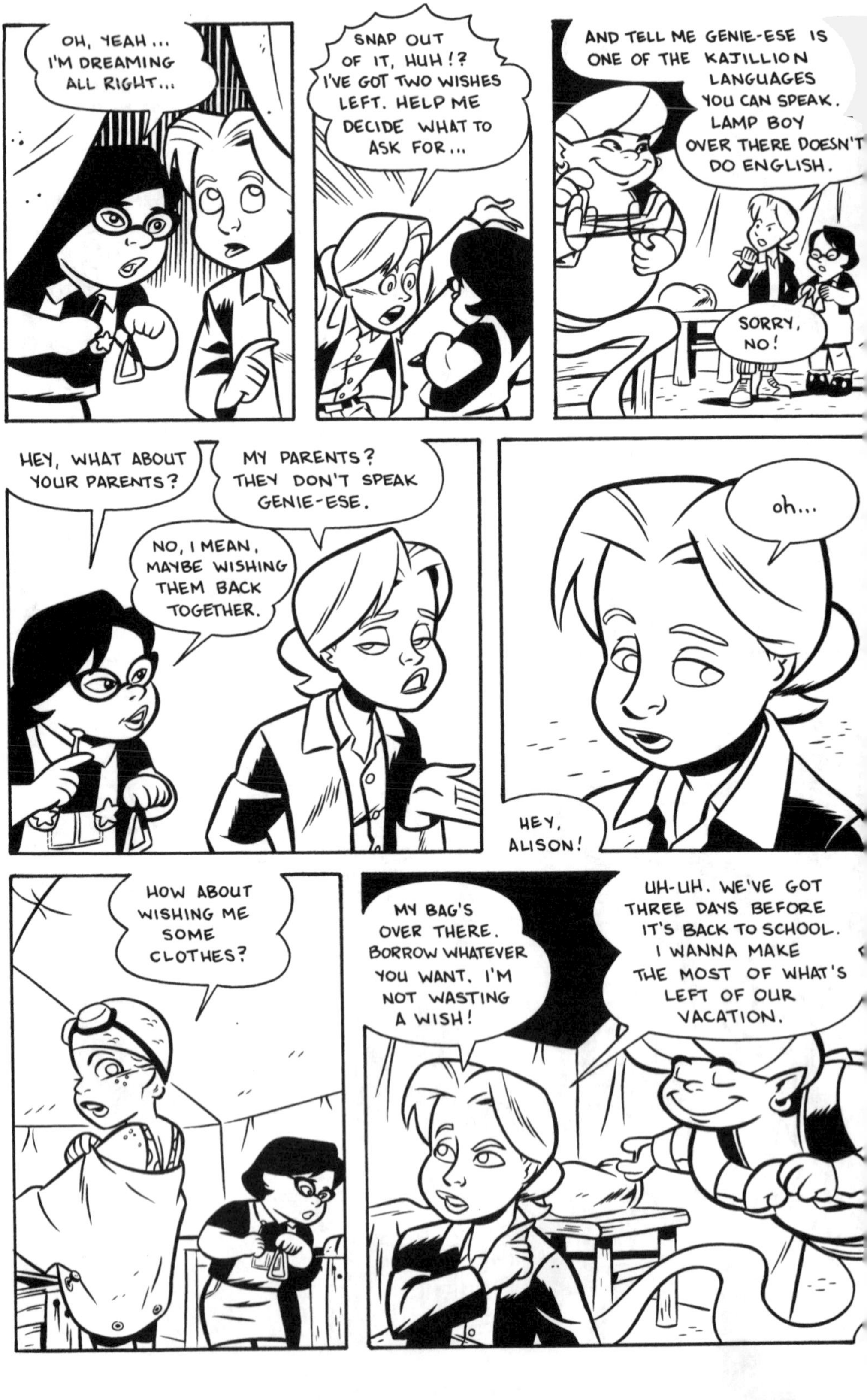
OH, YEAH... I'M DREAMING ALL RIGHT...
SNAP OUT OF IT, HUH!? I'VE GOT TWO WISHES LEFT. HELP ME DECIDE WHAT TO ASK FOR...
AND TELL ME GENIE-ESE IS ONE OF THE KAJILLION LANGUAGES YOU CAN SPEAK. LAMP BOY OVER THERE DOESN'T DO ENGLISH.
SORRY, NO!
HEY, WHAT ABOUT YOUR PARENTS?
MY PARENTS? THEY DON'T SPEAK GENIE-ESE.
NO, I MEAN, MAYBE WISHING THEM BACK TOGETHER.
oh...
HEY, ALISON!
HOW ABOUT WISHING ME SOME CLOTHES?
MY BAG'S OVER THERE. BORROW WHATEVER YOU WANT. I'M NOT WASTING A WISH!
UH-UH. WE'VE GOT THREE DAYS BEFORE IT'S BACK TO SCHOOL. I WANNA MAKE THE MOST OF WHAT'S LEFT OF OUR VACATION.

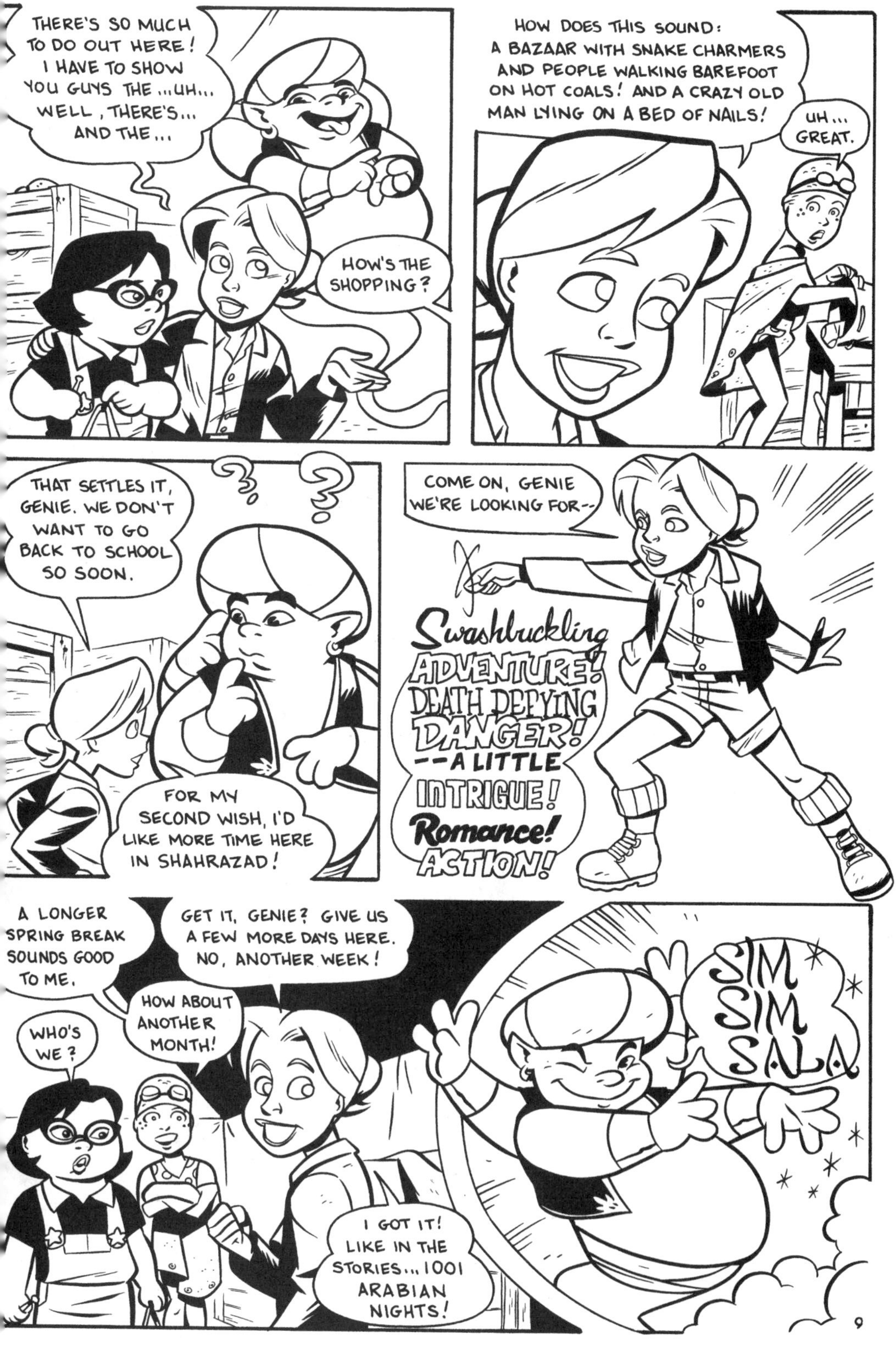

THERE'S SO MUCH TO DO OUT HERE! I HAVE TO SHOW YOU GUYS THE ...UH... WELL, THERE'S... AND THE...
HOW'S THE SHOPPING?
HOW DOES THIS SOUND: A BAZAAR WITH SNAKE CHARMERS AND PEOPLE WALKING BAREFOOT ON HOT COALS! AND A CRAZY OLD MAN LYING ON A BED OF NAILS!
UH... GREAT.
THAT SETTLES IT, GENIE. WE DON'T WANT TO GO BACK TO SCHOOL SO SOON.
FOR MY SECOND WISH, I'D LIKE MORE TIME HERE IN SHAHRAZAD!
COME ON, GENIE WE'RE LOOKING FOR--
Swashbuckling ADVENTURE! DEATH DEFYING DANGER! --A LITTLE INTRIGUE! Romance! ACTION!
A LONGER SPRING BREAK SOUNDS GOOD TO ME.
GET IT, GENIE? GIVE US A FEW MORE DAYS HERE. NO, ANOTHER WEEK!
WHO'S WE?
HOW ABOUT ANOTHER MONTH!
I GOT IT! LIKE IN THE STORIES... 1001 ARABIAN NIGHTS!
SIM SIM SALA

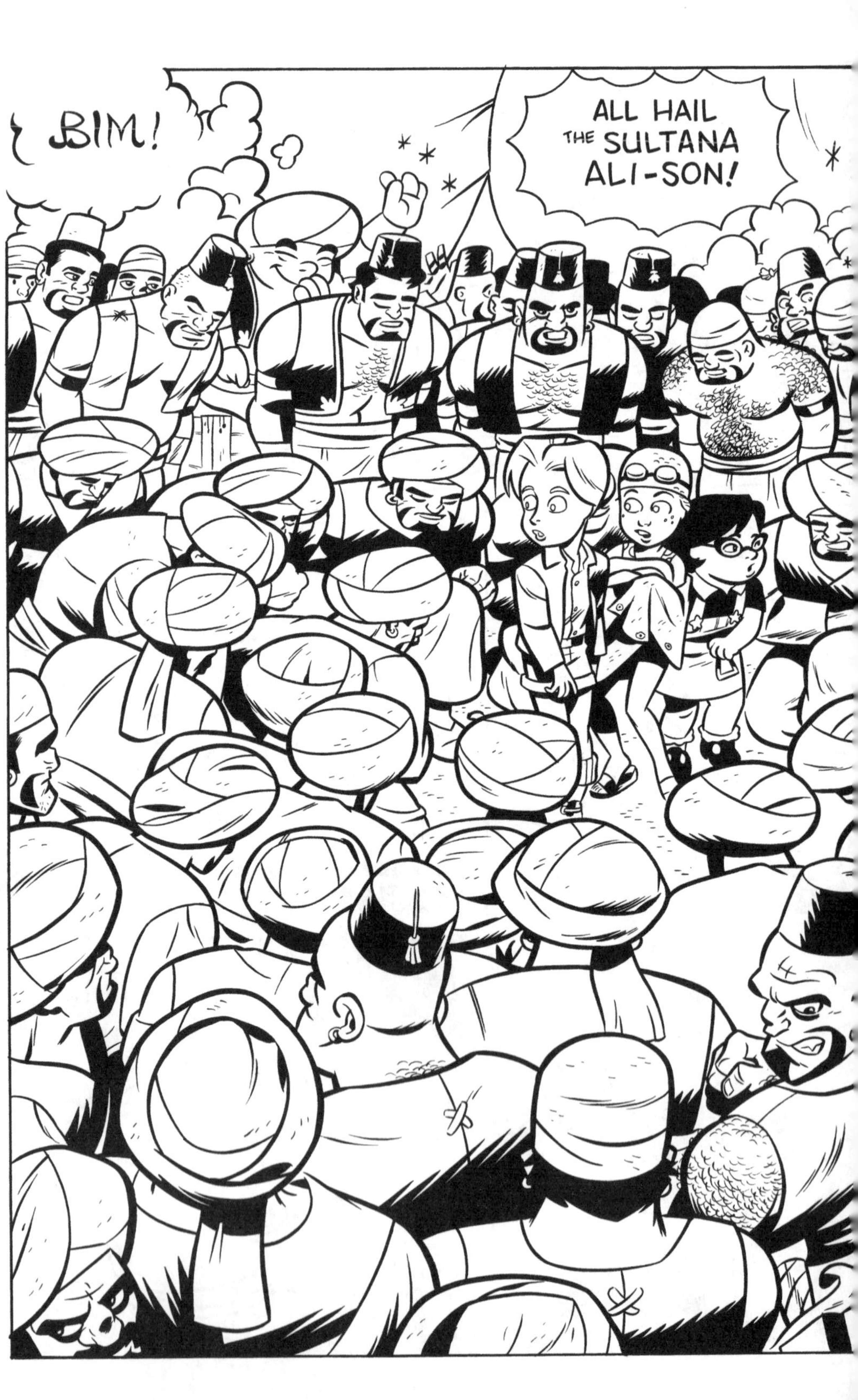
BIM!
ALL HAIL THE SULTANA ALI-SON!

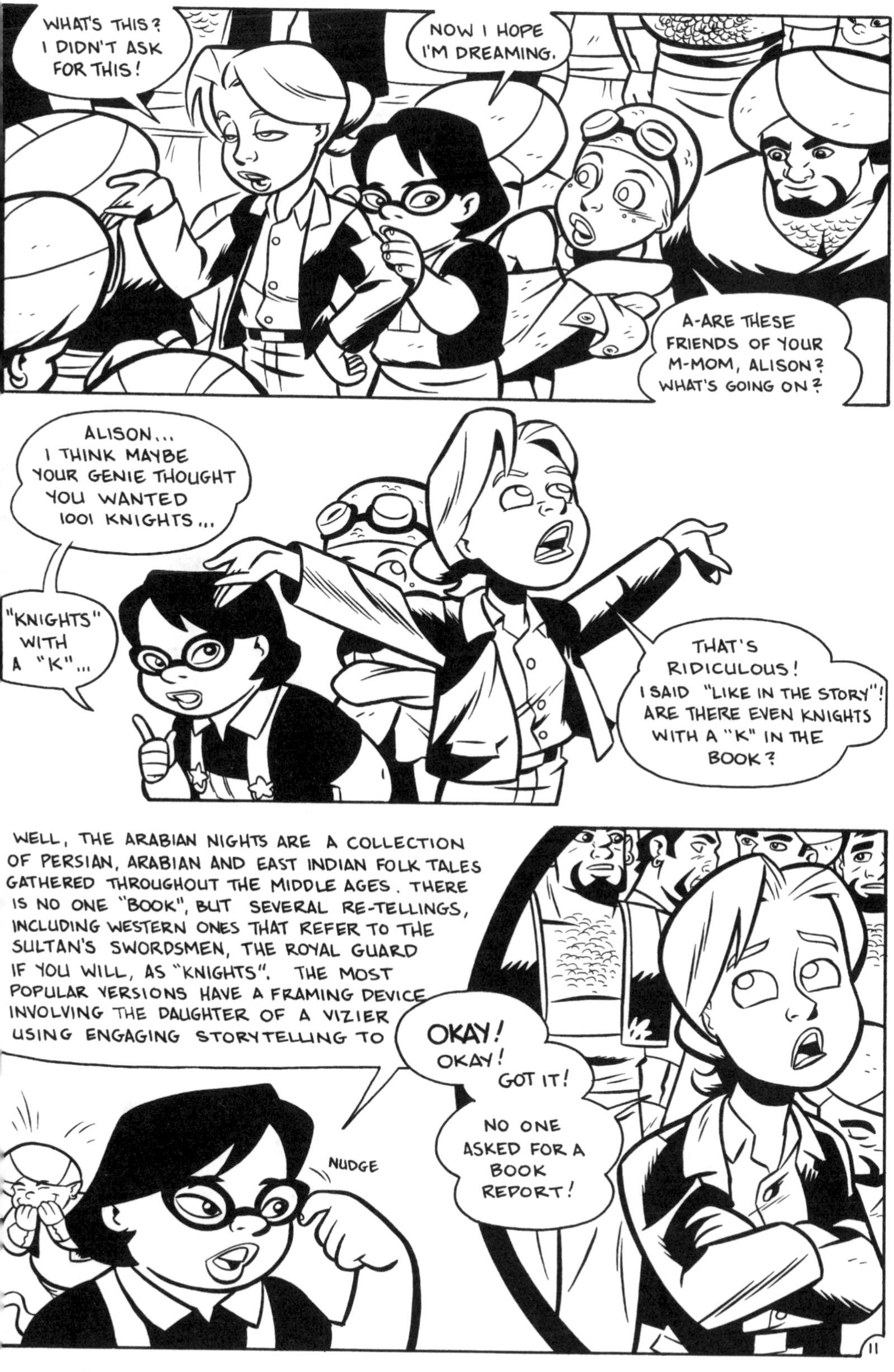
WHAT'S THIS? I DIDN'T ASK FOR THIS!
NOW I HOPE I'M DREAMING.
A-ARE THESE FRIENDS OF YOUR M-MOM, ALISON? WHAT'S GOING ON?
ALISON... I THINK MAYBE YOUR GENIE THOUGHT YOU WANTED 1001 KNIGHTS...
"KNIGHTS" WITH A "K"...
THAT'S RIDICULOUS! I SAID "LIKE IN THE STORY"! ARE THERE EVEN KNIGHTS WITH A "K" IN THE BOOK?
WELL, THE ARABIAN NIGHTS ARE A COLLECTION OF PERSIAN, ARABIAN AND EAST INDIAN FOLK TALES GATHERED THROUGHOUT THE MIDDLE AGES. THERE IS NO ONE "BOOK", BUT SEVERAL RE-TELLINGS, INCLUDING WESTERN ONES THAT REFER TO THE SULTAN'S SWORDSMEN, THE ROYAL GUARD IF YOU WILL, AS "KNIGHTS". THE MOST POPULAR VERSIONS HAVE A FRAMING DEVICE INVOLVING THE DAUGHTER OF A VIZIER USING ENGAGING STORYTELLING TO
OKAY! OKAY! GOT IT!
NO ONE ASKED FOR A BOOK REPORT!
NUDGE

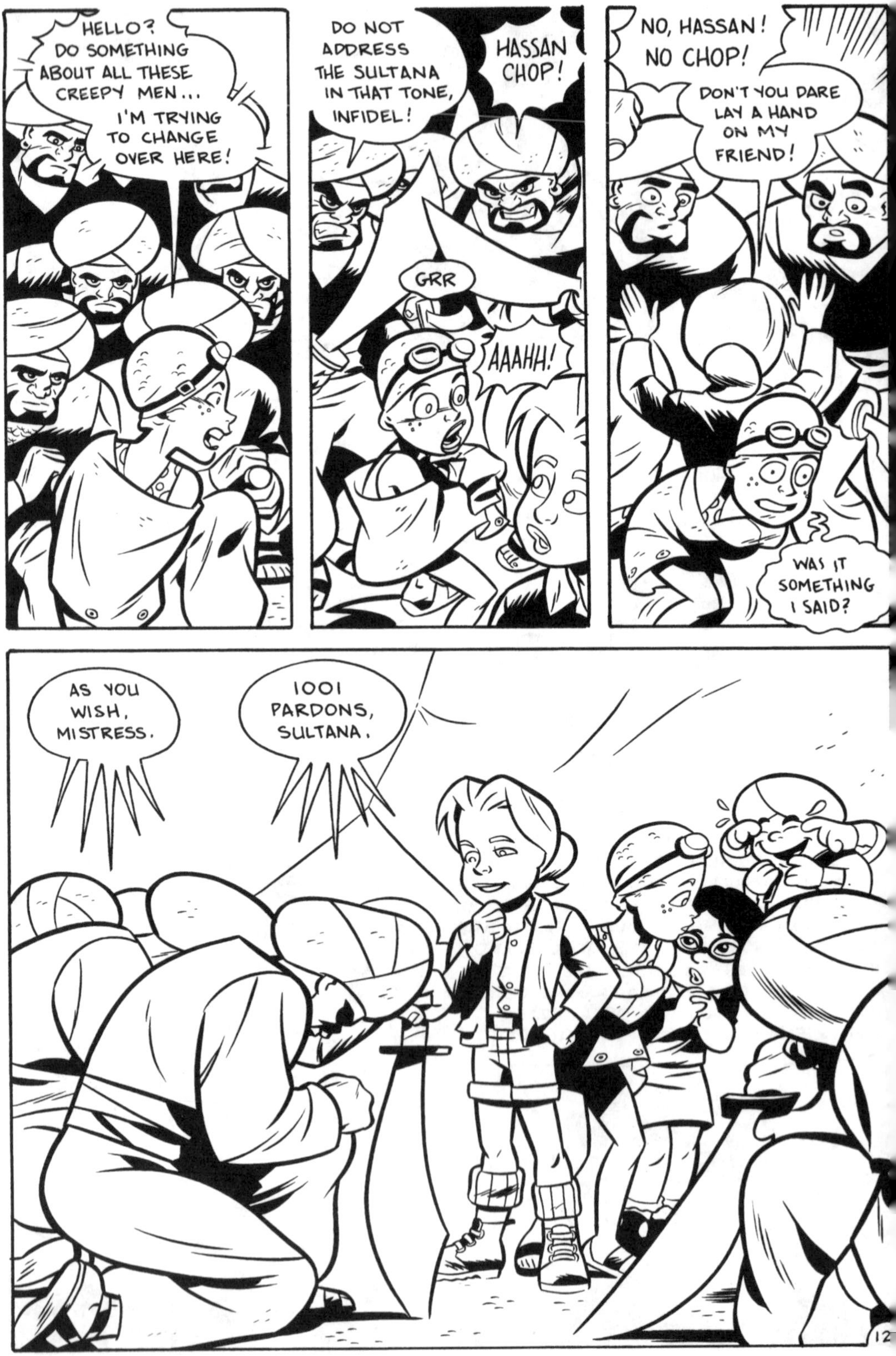
HELLO? DO SOMETHING ABOUT ALL THESE CREEPY MEN...
I'M TRYING TO CHANGE OVER HERE!
DO NOT ADDRESS THE SULTANA IN THAT TONE, INFIDEL!
HASSAN CHOP!
GRR
AAAHH!
NO, HASSAN! NO CHOP!
DON'T YOU DARE LAY A HAND ON MY FRIEND!
WAS IT SOMETHING I SAID?
AS YOU WISH, MISTRESS.
1001 PARDONS, SULTANA.

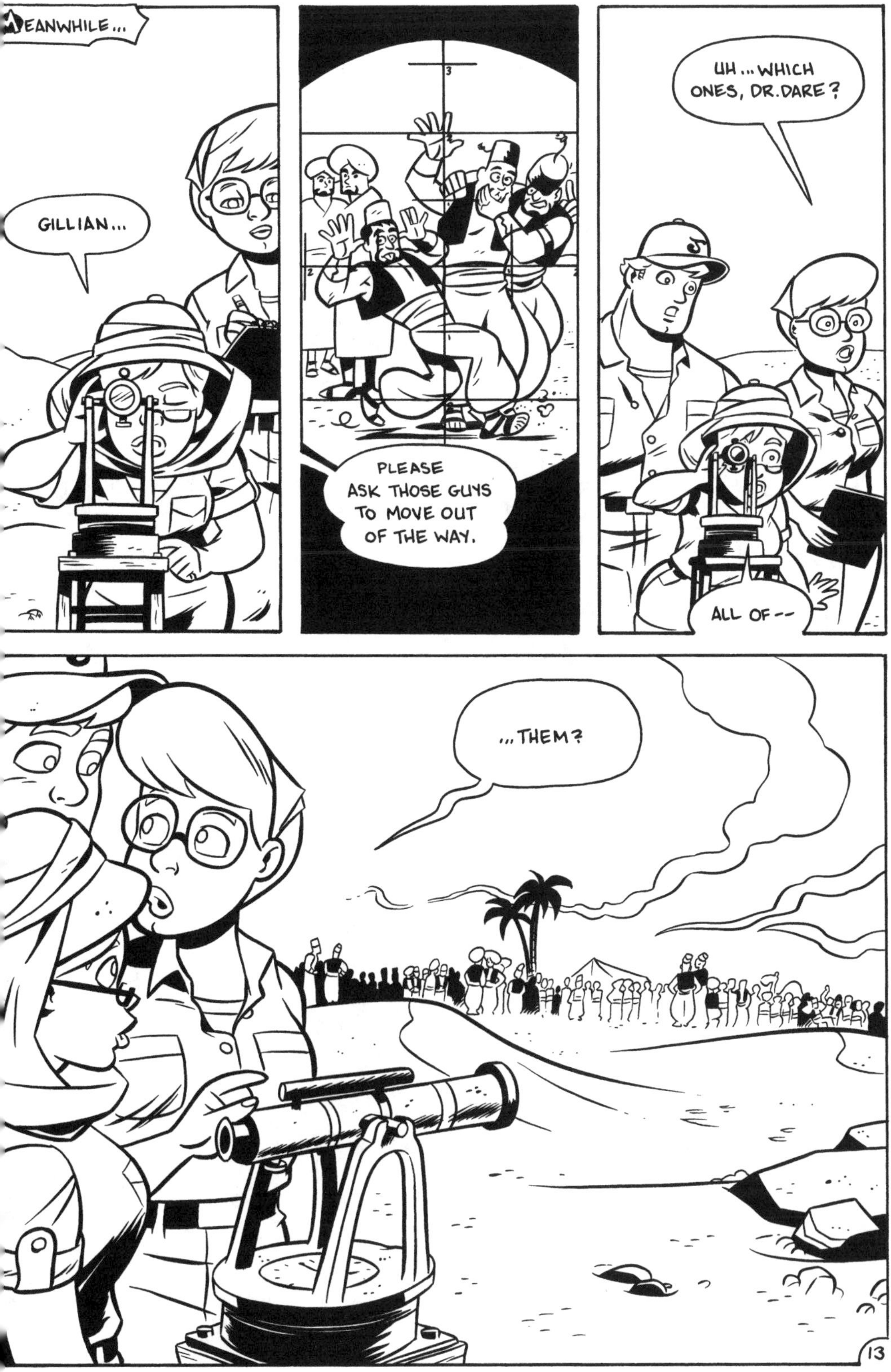
MEANWHILE...
GILLIAN...
PLEASE ASK THOSE GUYS TO MOVE OUT OF THE WAY.
UH... WHICH ONES, DR. DARE?
ALL OF--
...THEM?

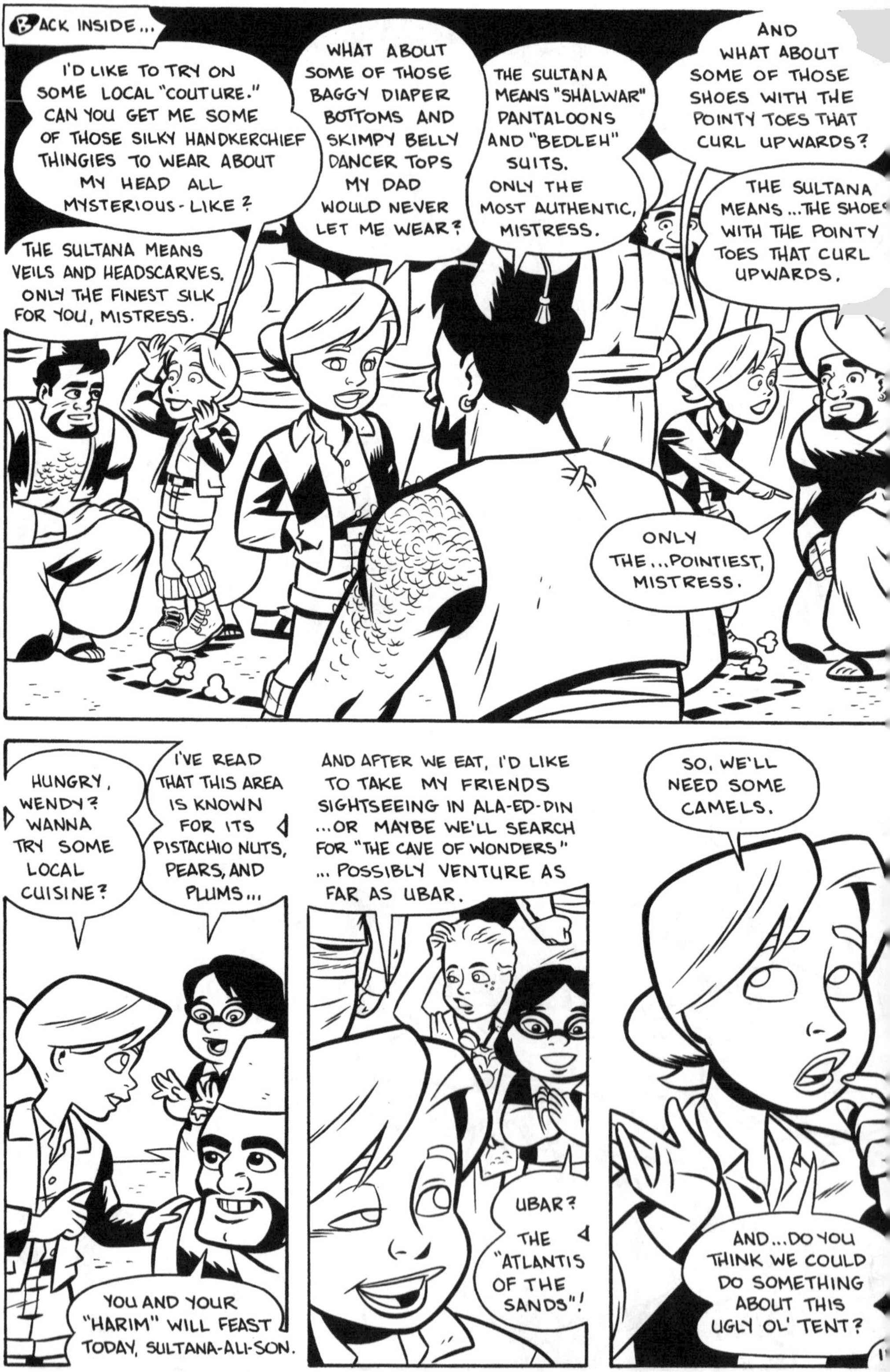
BACK INSIDE...
I'D LIKE TO TRY ON SOME LOCAL "COUTURE." CAN YOU GET ME SOME OF THOSE SILKY HANDKERCHIEF THINGIES TO WEAR ABOUT MY HEAD ALL MYSTERIOUS-LIKE?
THE SULTANA MEANS VEILS AND HEADSCARVES. ONLY THE FINEST SILK FOR YOU, MISTRESS.
WHAT ABOUT SOME OF THOSE BAGGY DIAPER BOTTOMS AND SKIMPY BELLY DANCER TOPS MY DAD WOULD NEVER LET ME WEAR?
THE SULTANA MEANS "SHALWAR" PANTALOONS AND "BEDLEH" SUITS. ONLY THE MOST AUTHENTIC, MISTRESS.
AND WHAT ABOUT SOME OF THOSE SHOES WITH THE POINTY TOES THAT CURL UPWARDS?
THE SULTANA MEANS...THE SHOES WITH THE POINTY TOES THAT CURL UPWARDS.
ONLY THE...POINTIEST, MISTRESS.
HUNGRY, WENDY? WANNA TRY SOME LOCAL CUISINE?
I'VE READ THAT THIS AREA IS KNOWN FOR ITS PISTACHIO NUTS, PEARS, AND PLUMS...
YOU AND YOUR "HARIM" WILL FEAST TODAY, SULTANA-ALI-SON.
AND AFTER WE EAT, I'D LIKE TO TAKE MY FRIENDS SIGHTSEEING IN ALA-ED-DIN ...OR MAYBE WE'LL SEARCH FOR "THE CAVE OF WONDERS" ... POSSIBLY VENTURE AS FAR AS UBAR.
UBAR? THE "ATLANTIS OF THE SANDS"!
SO, WE'LL NEED SOME CAMELS.
AND...DO YOU THINK WE COULD DO SOMETHING ABOUT THIS UGLY OL' TENT?

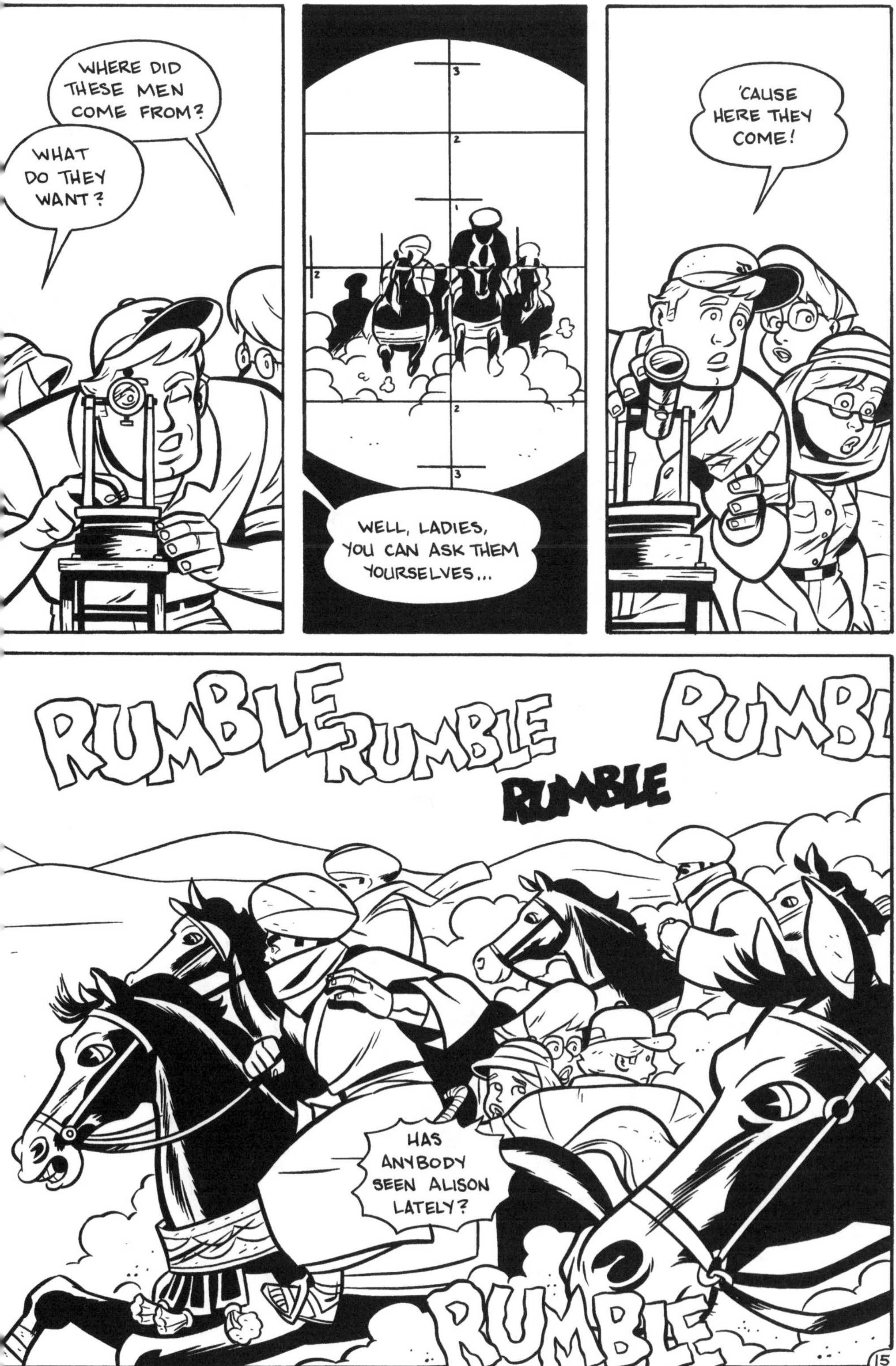
WHERE DID THESE MEN COME FROM?
WHAT DO THEY WANT?
WELL, LADIES, YOU CAN ASK THEM YOURSELVES...
'CAUSE HERE THEY COME!
RUMBLE RUMBLE RUMBLE
RUMBLE
HAS ANYBODY SEEN ALISON LATELY?
RUMBLE

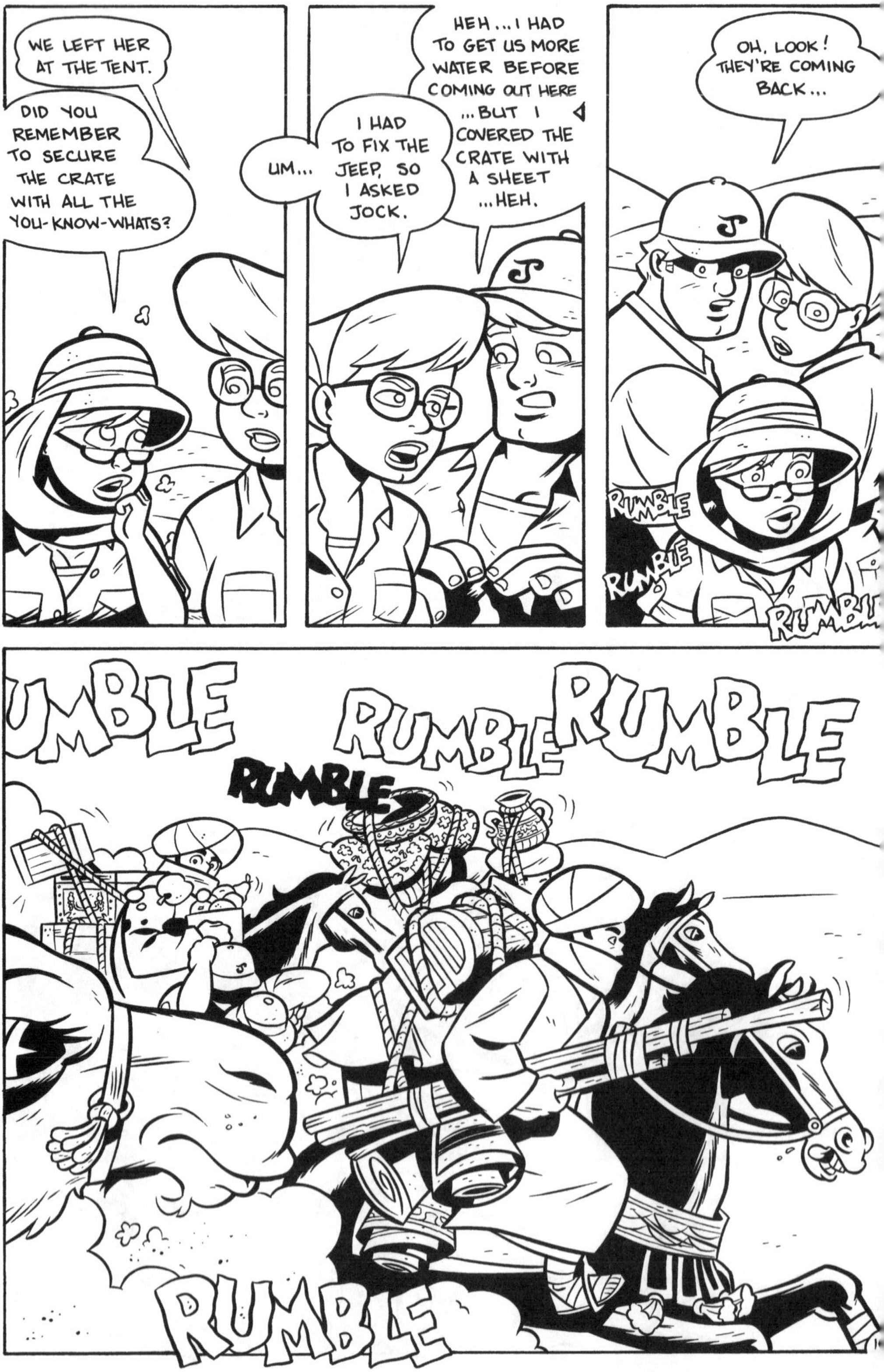

WE LEFT HER AT THE TENT.
DID YOU REMEMBER TO SECURE THE CRATE WITH ALL THE YOU-KNOW-WHATS?
UM...
I HAD TO FIX THE JEEP, SO I ASKED JOCK.
HEH... I HAD TO GET US MORE WATER BEFORE COMING OUT HERE
...BUT I COVERED THE CRATE WITH A SHEET ...HEH.
OH, LOOK! THEY'RE COMING BACK...
RUMBLE
RUMBLE
RUMBLE
RUMBLE
RUMBLE
RUMBLE
RUMBLE
RUMBLE
RUMBLE

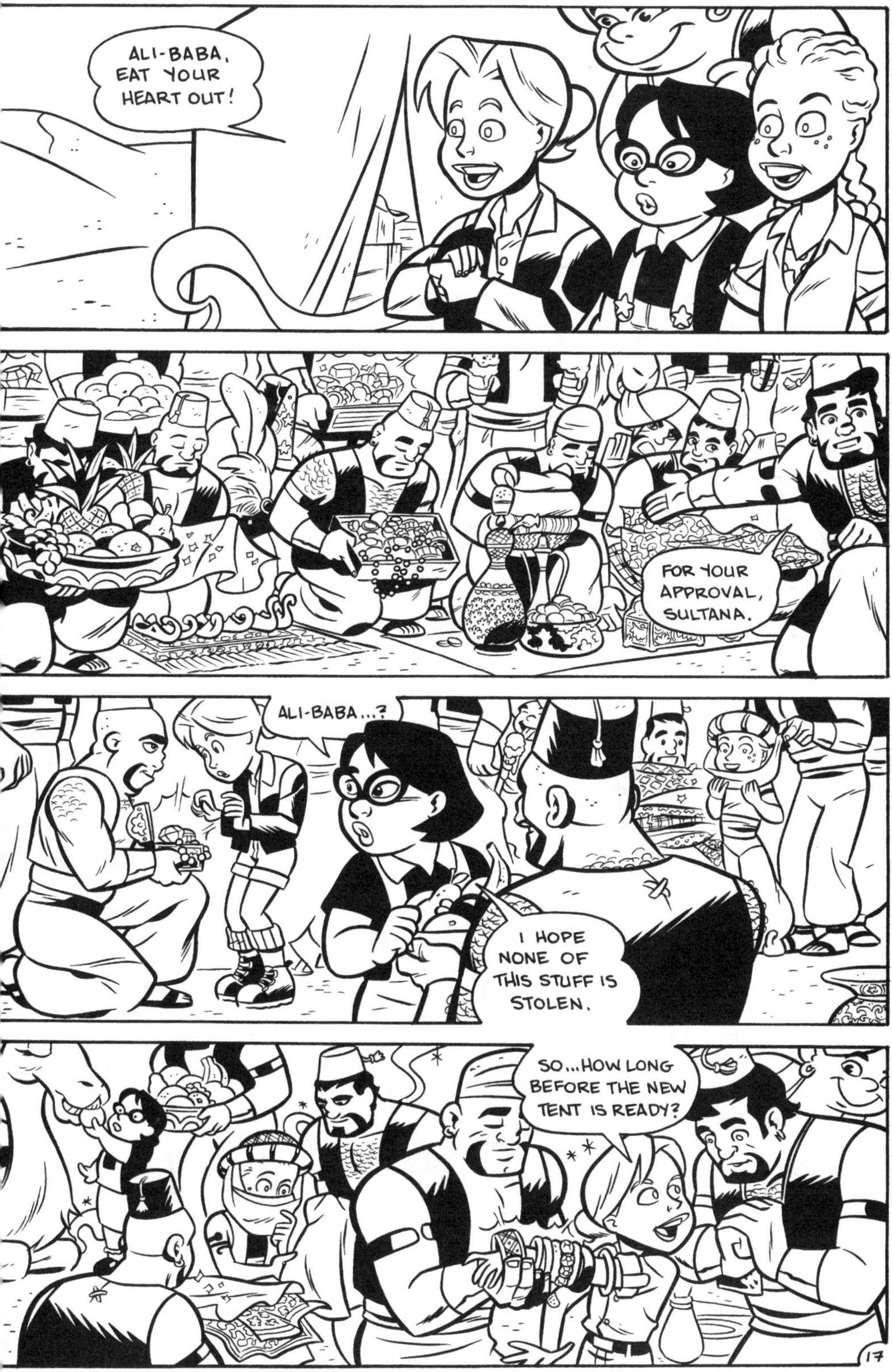
ALI-BABA, EAT YOUR HEART OUT!
FOR YOUR APPROVAL, SULTANA.
ALI-BABA...?
I HOPE NONE OF THIS STUFF IS STOLEN.
SO...HOW LONG BEFORE THE NEW TENT IS READY?

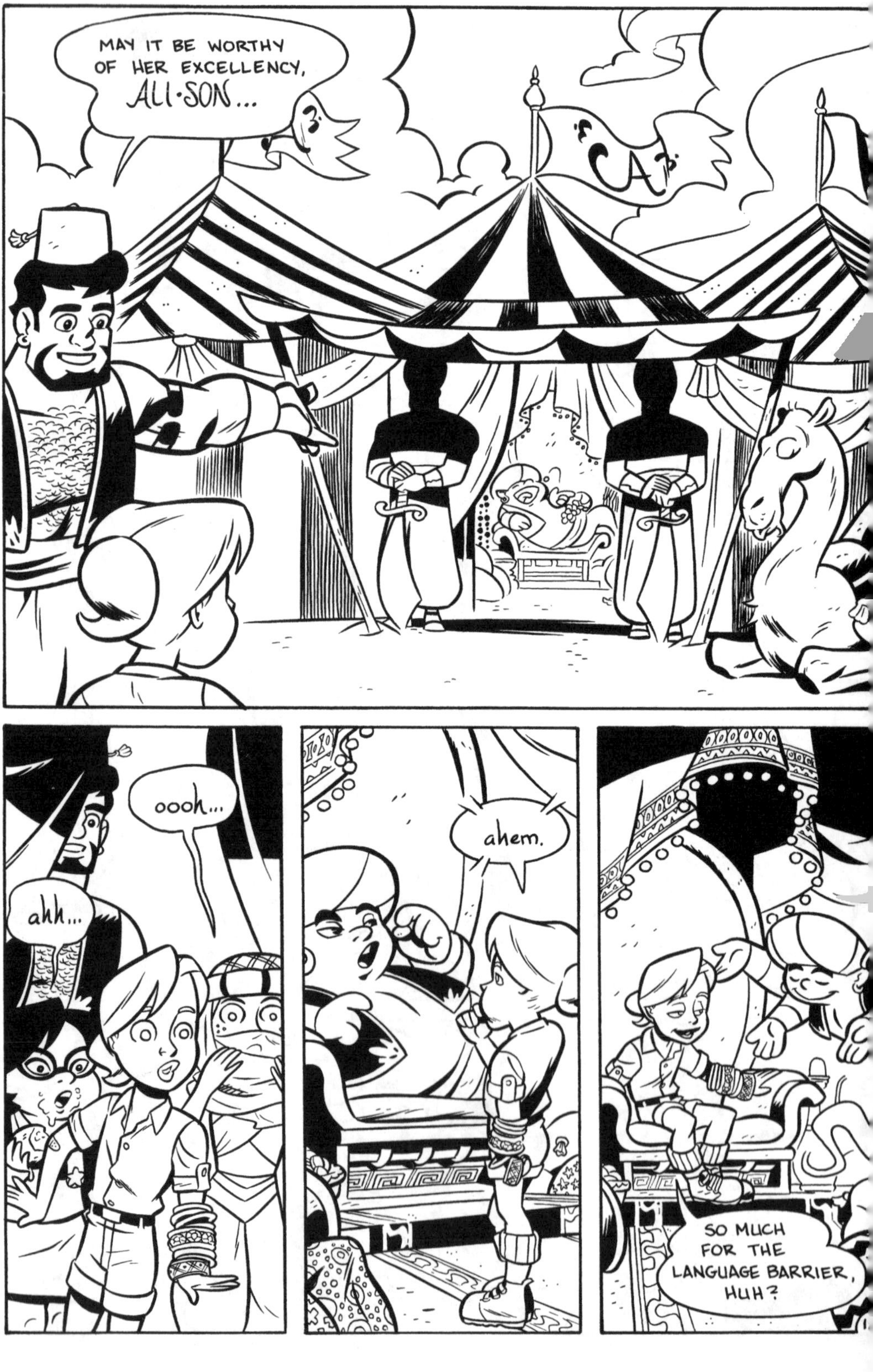
MAY IT BE WORTHY OF HER EXCELLENCY, ALI-SON...
oooh...
ahh...
ahem.
SO MUCH FOR THE LANGUAGE BARRIER, HUH?

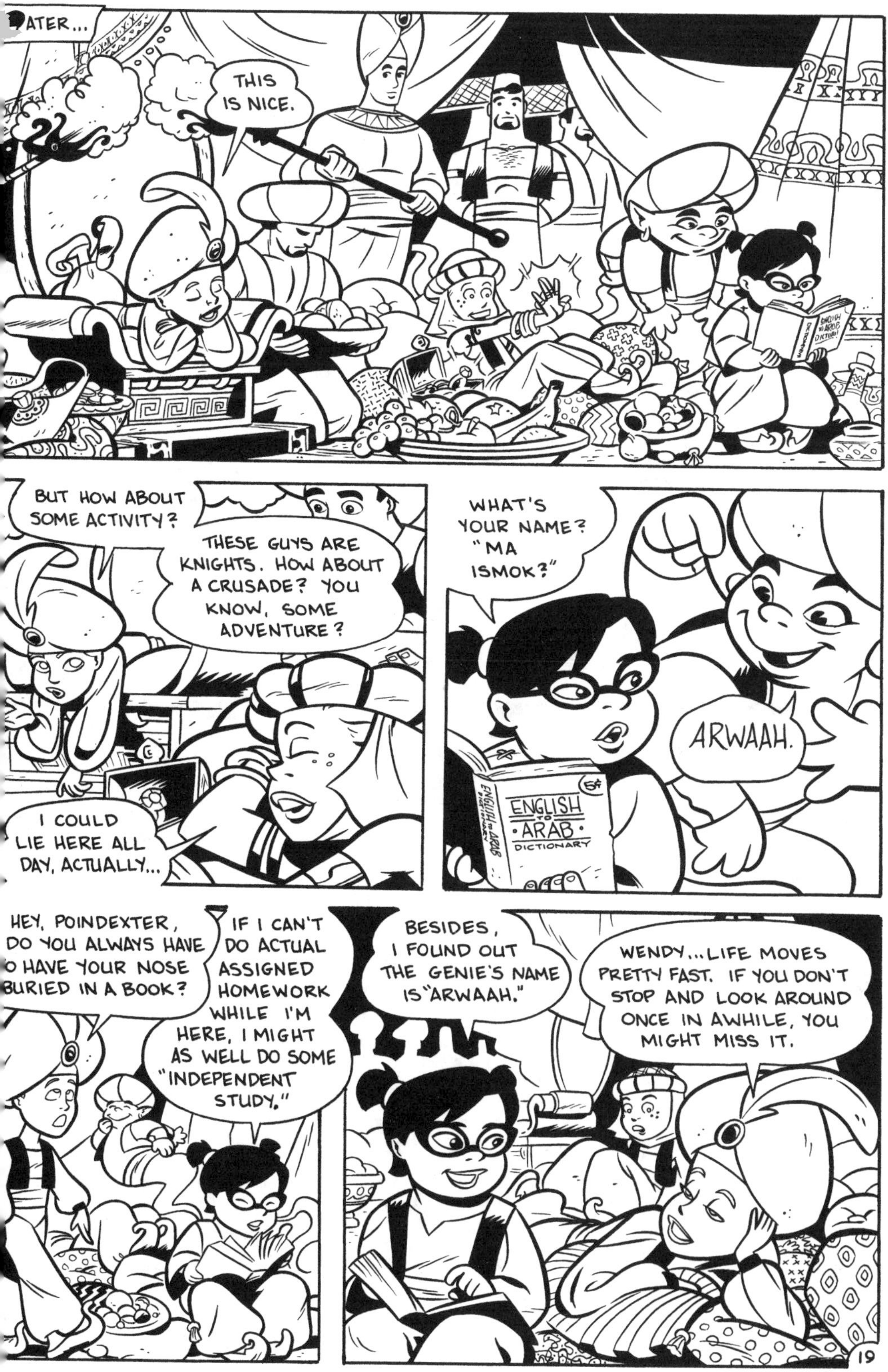
LATER...
THIS IS NICE.
BUT HOW ABOUT SOME ACTIVITY?
THESE GUYS ARE KNIGHTS. HOW ABOUT A CRUSADE? YOU KNOW, SOME ADVENTURE?
I COULD LIE HERE ALL DAY, ACTUALLY...
WHAT'S YOUR NAME? "MA ISMOK?"
ARWAAH.
ENGLISH TO ARAB DICTIONARY
5¢
HEY, POINDEXTER, DO YOU ALWAYS HAVE TO HAVE YOUR NOSE BURIED IN A BOOK?
IF I CAN'T DO ACTUAL ASSIGNED HOMEWORK WHILE I'M HERE, I MIGHT AS WELL DO SOME "INDEPENDENT STUDY."
BESIDES, I FOUND OUT THE GENIE'S NAME IS "ARWAAH."
WENDY...LIFE MOVES PRETTY FAST. IF YOU DON'T STOP AND LOOK AROUND ONCE IN AWHILE, YOU MIGHT MISS IT.

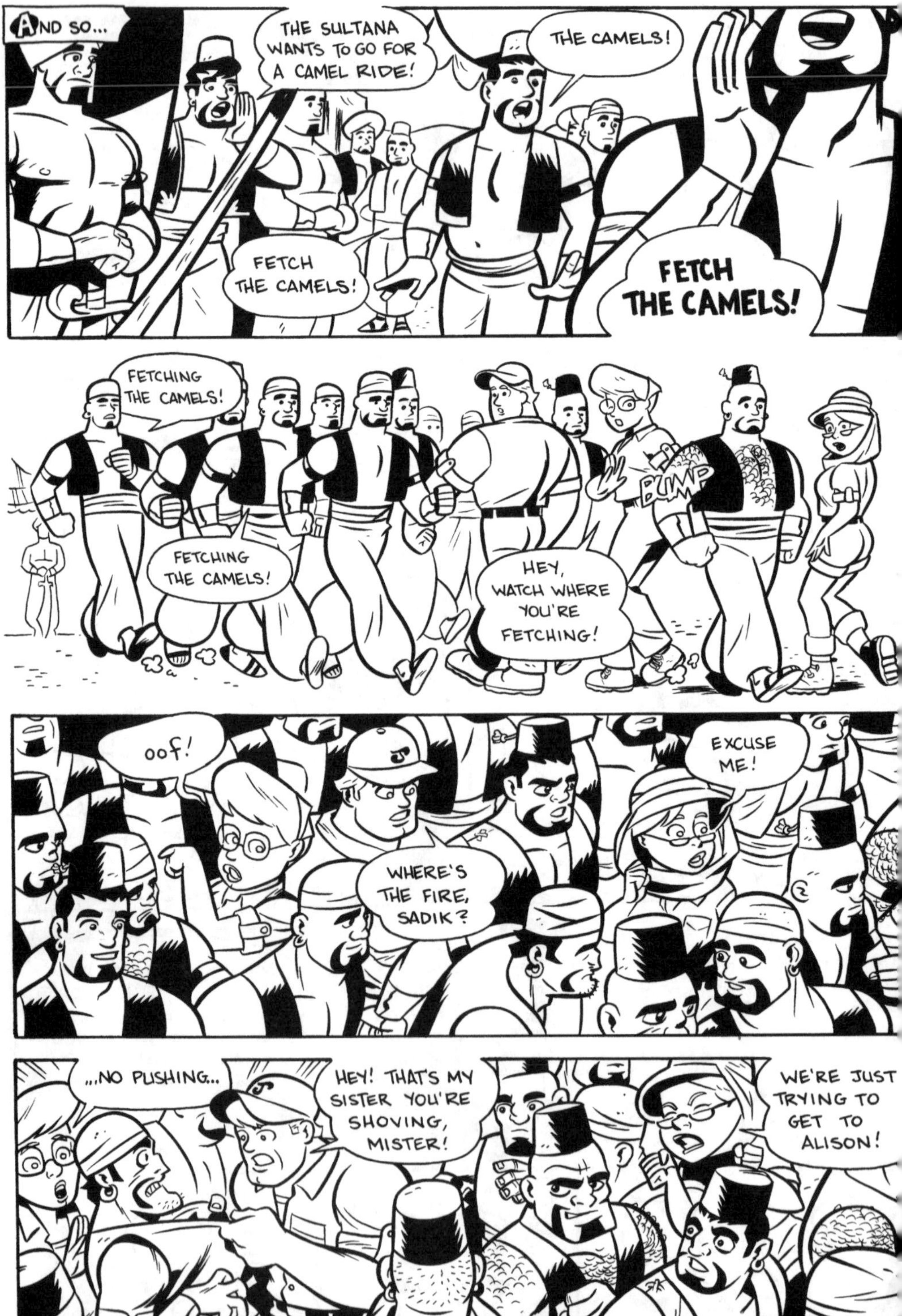
AND SO...
THE SULTANA WANTS TO GO FOR A CAMEL RIDE!
THE CAMELS!
FETCH THE CAMELS!
FETCH THE CAMELS!
FETCHING THE CAMELS!
FETCHING THE CAMELS!
BUMP
HEY, WATCH WHERE YOU'RE FETCHING!
oof!
EXCUSE ME!
WHERE'S THE FIRE, SADIK?
...NO PUSHING...
HEY! THAT'S MY SISTER YOU'RE SHOVING, MISTER!
WE'RE JUST TRYING TO GET TO ALISON!

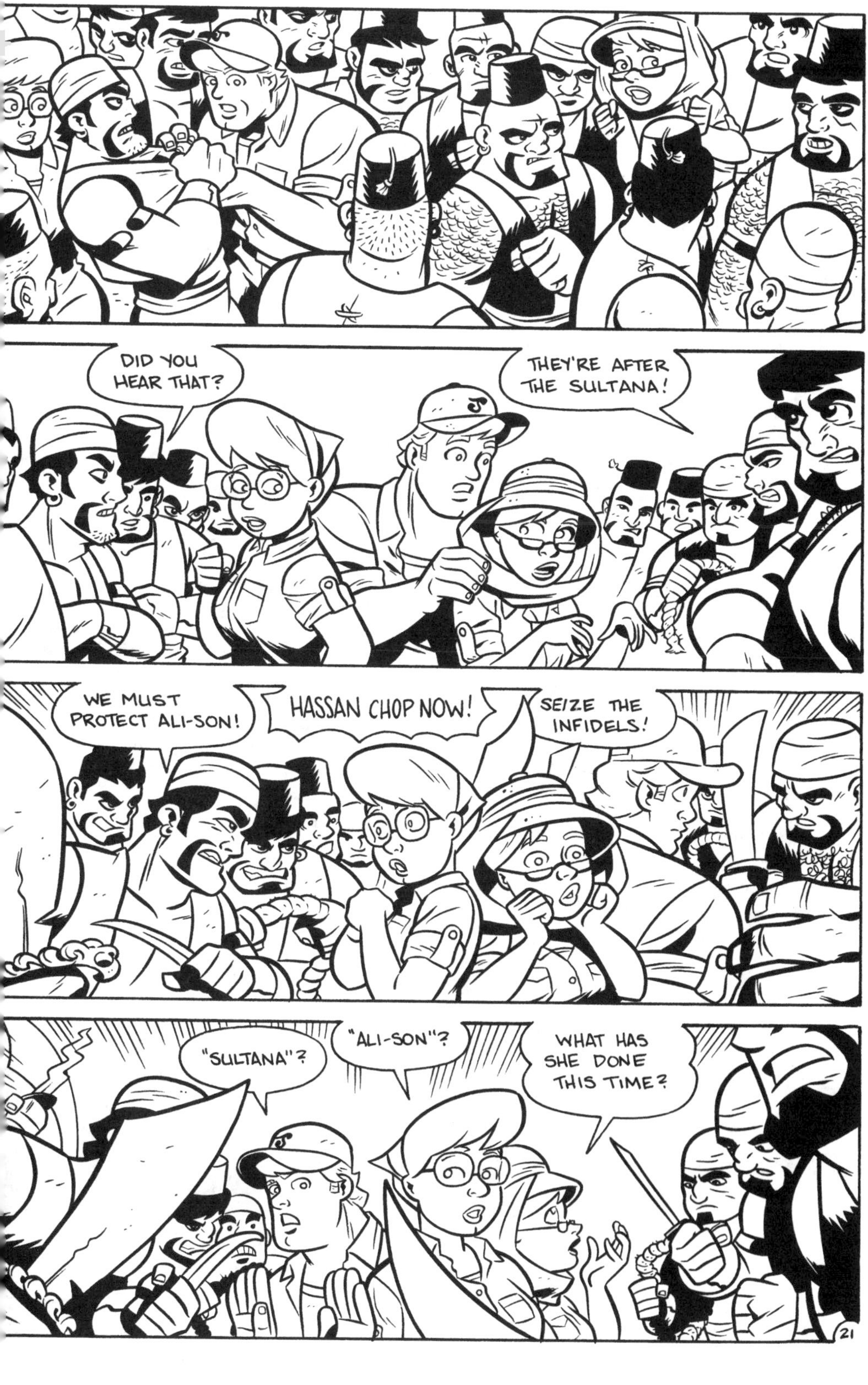
DID YOU HEAR THAT?
THEY'RE AFTER THE SULTANA!
WE MUST PROTECT ALI-SON!
HASSAN CHOP NOW!
SEIZE THE INFIDELS!
"SULTANA"?
"ALI-SON"?
WHAT HAS SHE DONE THIS TIME?

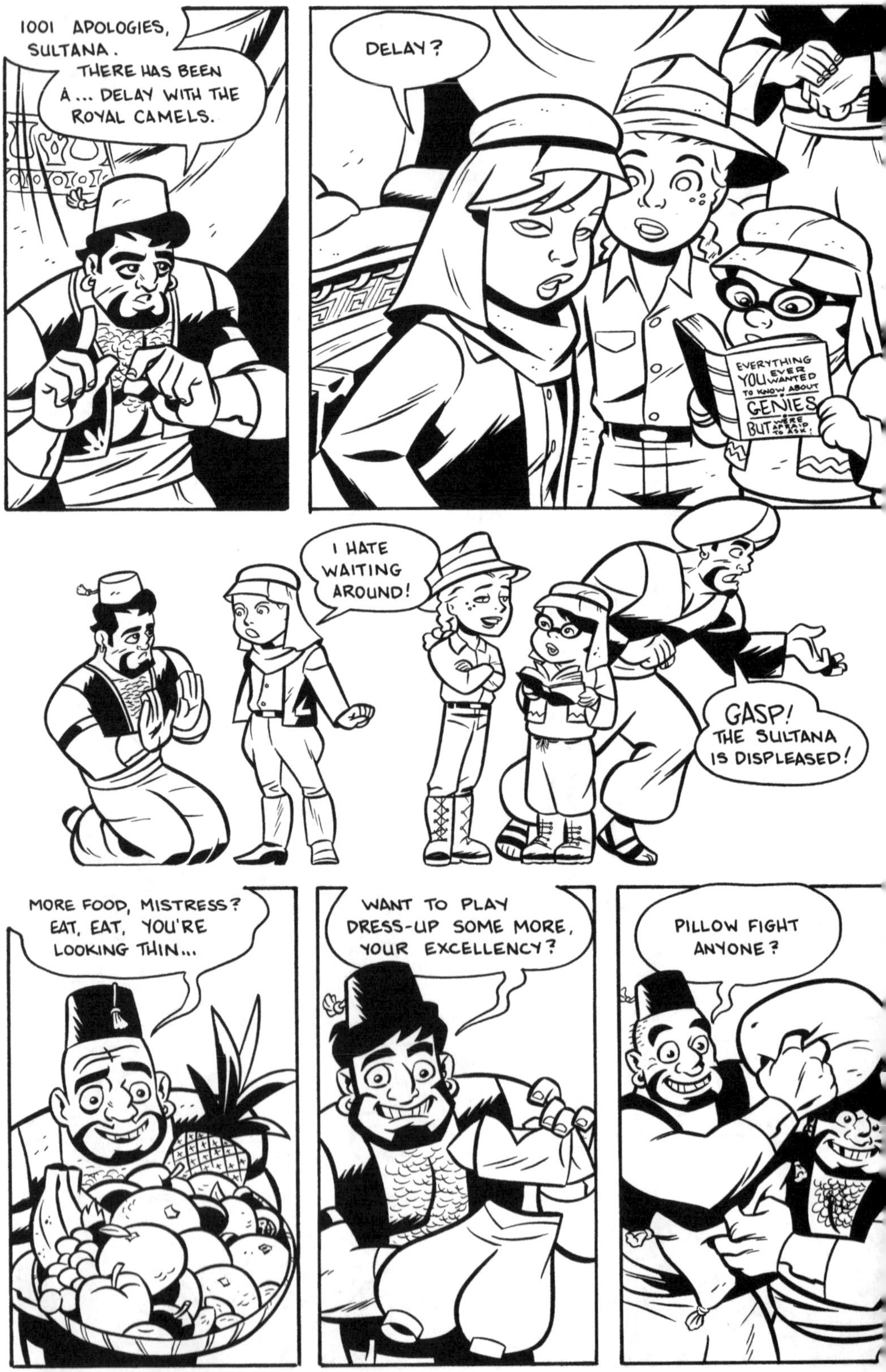
1001 APOLOGIES, SULTANA.
THERE HAS BEEN A... DELAY WITH THE ROYAL CAMELS.
DELAY?
EVERYTHING YOU EVER WANTED TO KNOW ABOUT GENIES BUT WERE AFRAID TO ASK!
I HATE WAITING AROUND!
GASP! THE SULTANA IS DISPLEASED!
MORE FOOD, MISTRESS? EAT, EAT, YOU'RE LOOKING THIN...
WANT TO PLAY DRESS-UP SOME MORE, YOUR EXCELLENCY?
PILLOW FIGHT ANYONE?

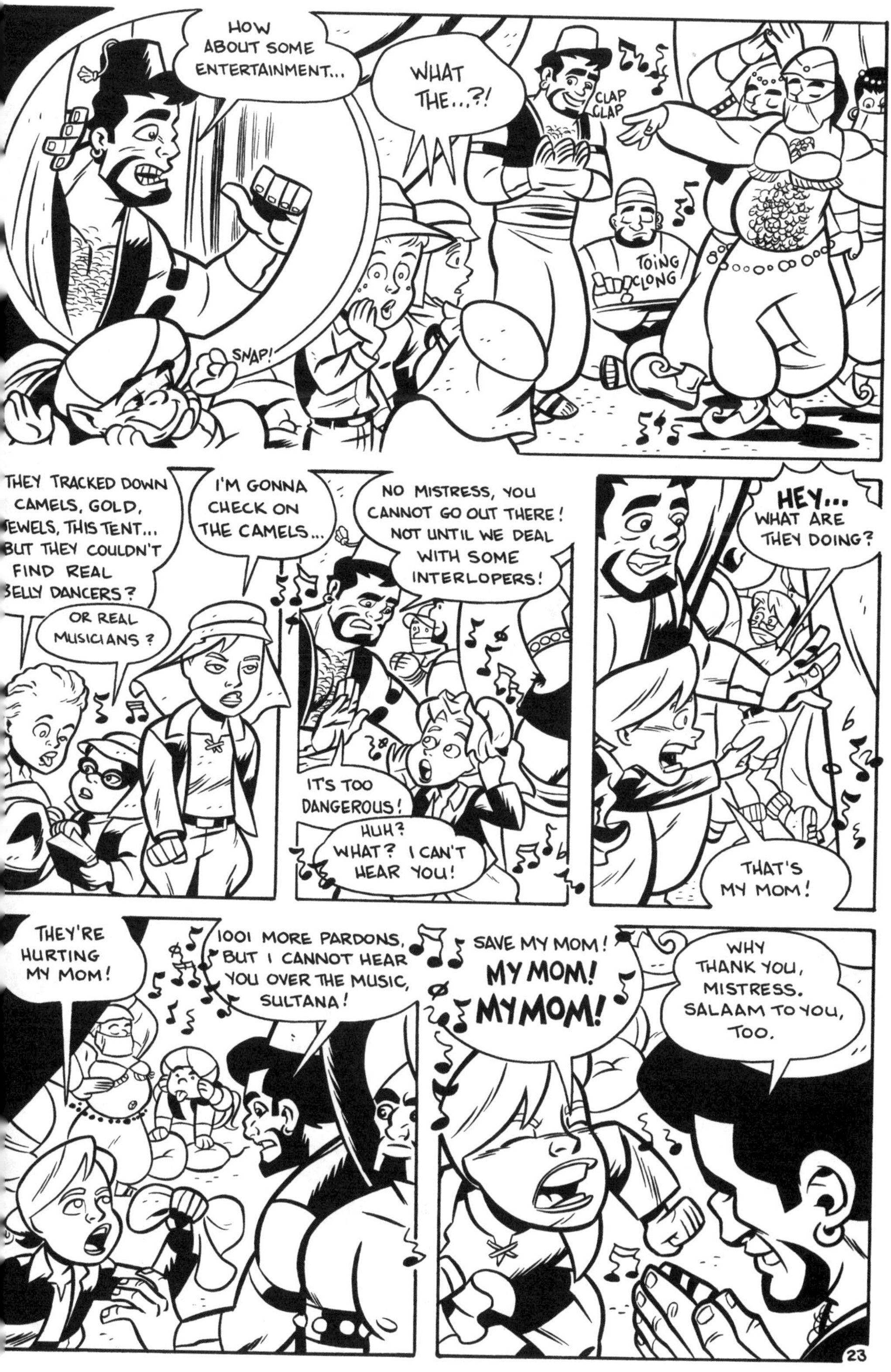
HOW ABOUT SOME ENTERTAINMENT...
WHAT THE...?!
CLAP CLAP
TOING CLONG
SNAP!
THEY TRACKED DOWN CAMELS, GOLD, EWELS, THIS TENT... BUT THEY COULDN'T FIND REAL ELLY DANCERS?
OR REAL MUSICIANS?
I'M GONNA CHECK ON THE CAMELS...
NO MISTRESS, YOU CANNOT GO OUT THERE! NOT UNTIL WE DEAL WITH SOME INTERLOPERS!
IT'S TOO DANGEROUS!
HUH? WHAT? I CAN'T HEAR YOU!
HEY... WHAT ARE THEY DOING?
THAT'S MY MOM!
THEY'RE HURTING MY MOM!
1001 MORE PARDONS, BUT I CANNOT HEAR YOU OVER THE MUSIC, SULTANA!
SAVE MY MOM! MY MOM! MY MOM!
WHY THANK YOU, MISTRESS. SALAAM TO YOU, TOO.

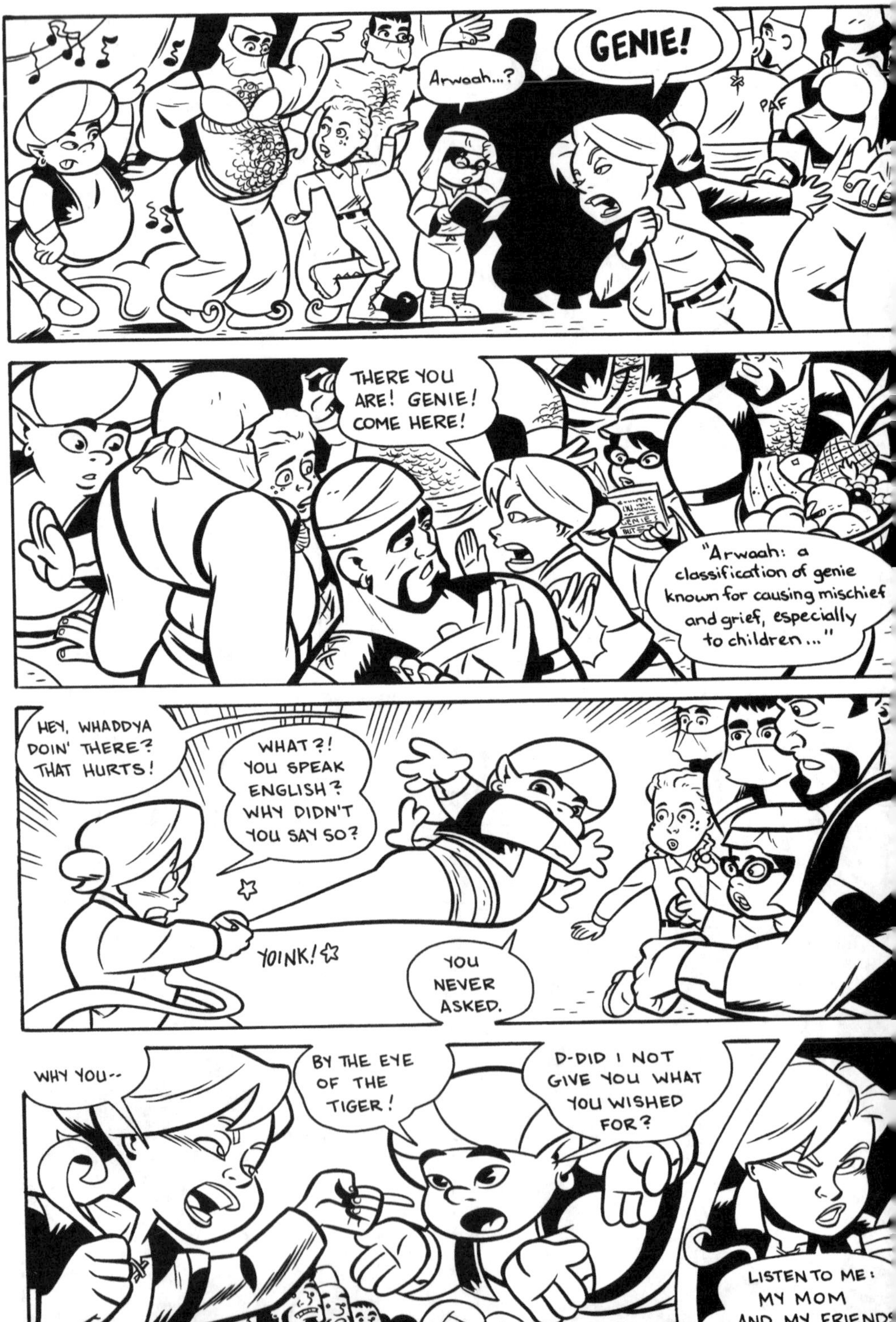
Arwoah...?
GENIE!
PAF
THERE YOU ARE! GENIE! COME HERE!
"Arwoah: a classification of genie known for causing mischief and grief, especially to children..."
HEY, WHADDYA DOIN' THERE? THAT HURTS!
WHAT?! YOU SPEAK ENGLISH? WHY DIDN'T YOU SAY SO?
YOINK!
YOU NEVER ASKED.
WHY YOU--
BY THE EYE OF THE TIGER!
D-DID I NOT GIVE YOU WHAT YOU WISHED FOR?
LISTEN TO ME: MY MOM AND MY FRIENDS ARE IN DANGER!

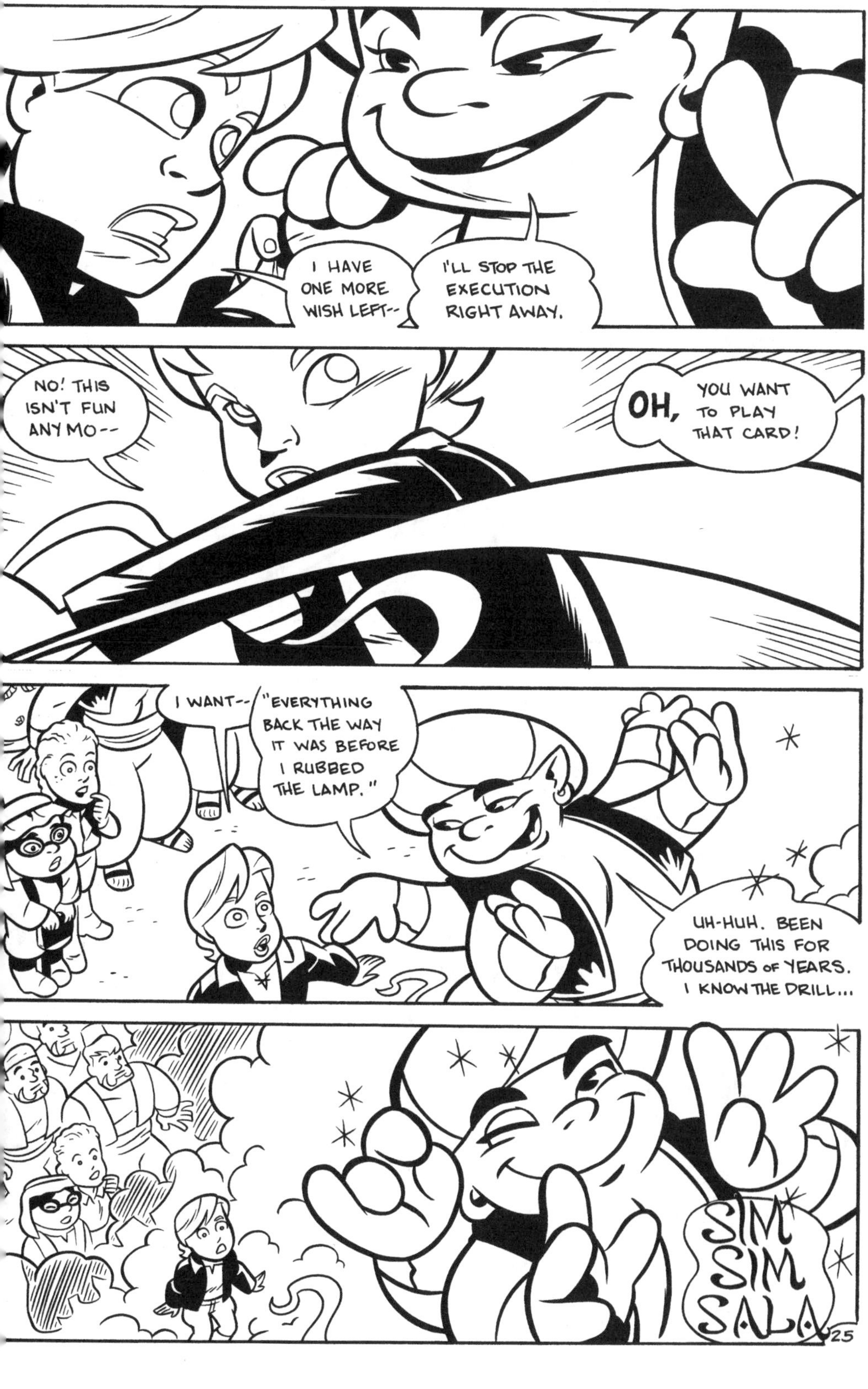
I HAVE ONE MORE WISH LEFT--
I'LL STOP THE EXECUTION RIGHT AWAY.
NO! THIS ISN'T FUN ANYMO--
OH, YOU WANT TO PLAY THAT CARD!
I WANT--
"EVERYTHING BACK THE WAY IT WAS BEFORE I RUBBED THE LAMP."
UH-HUH. BEEN DOING THIS FOR THOUSANDS OF YEARS. I KNOW THE DRILL...
SIM SIM SALA

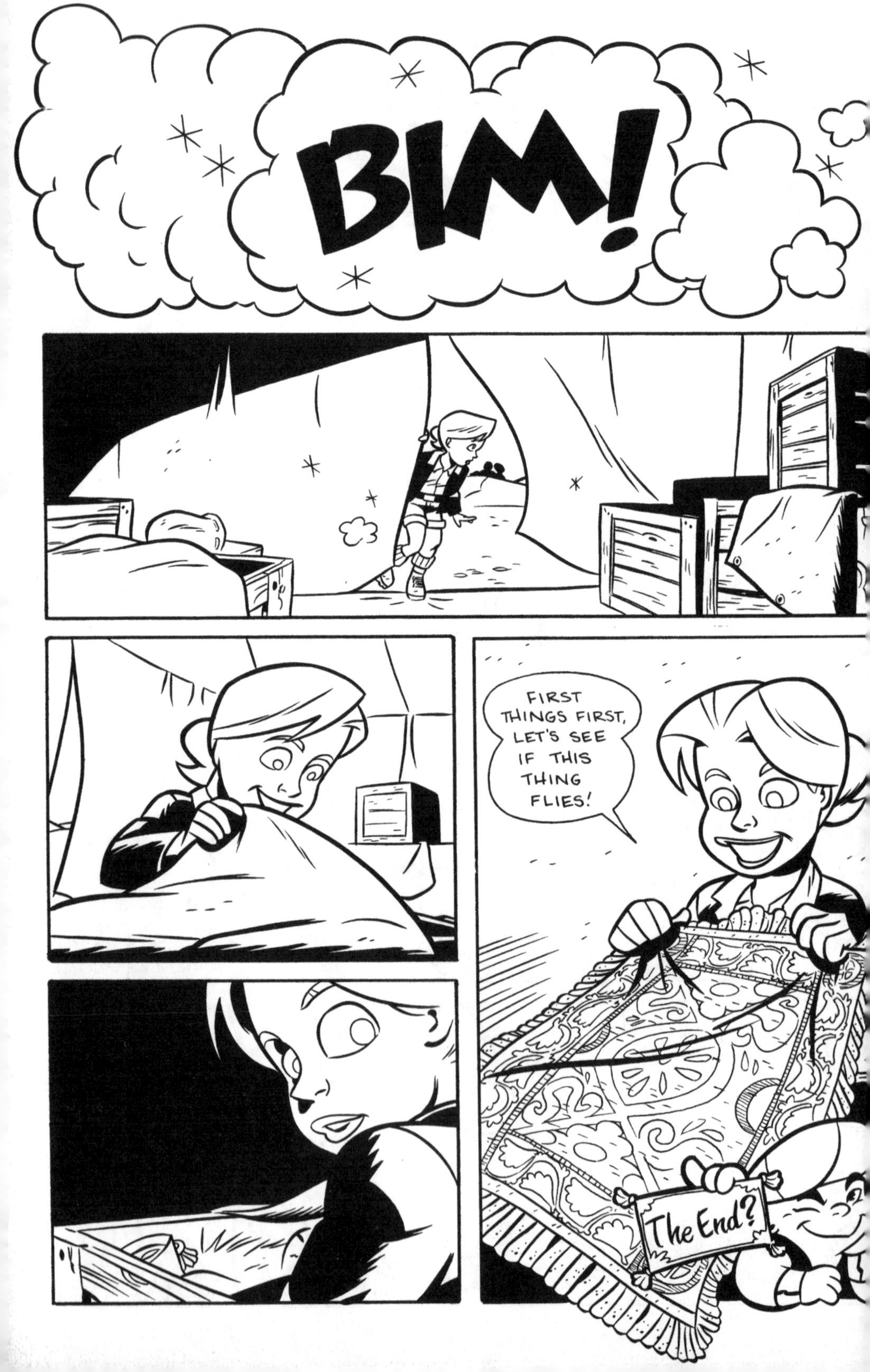
BIM!
FIRST THINGS FIRST, LET'S SEE IF THIS THING FLIES!
The End?

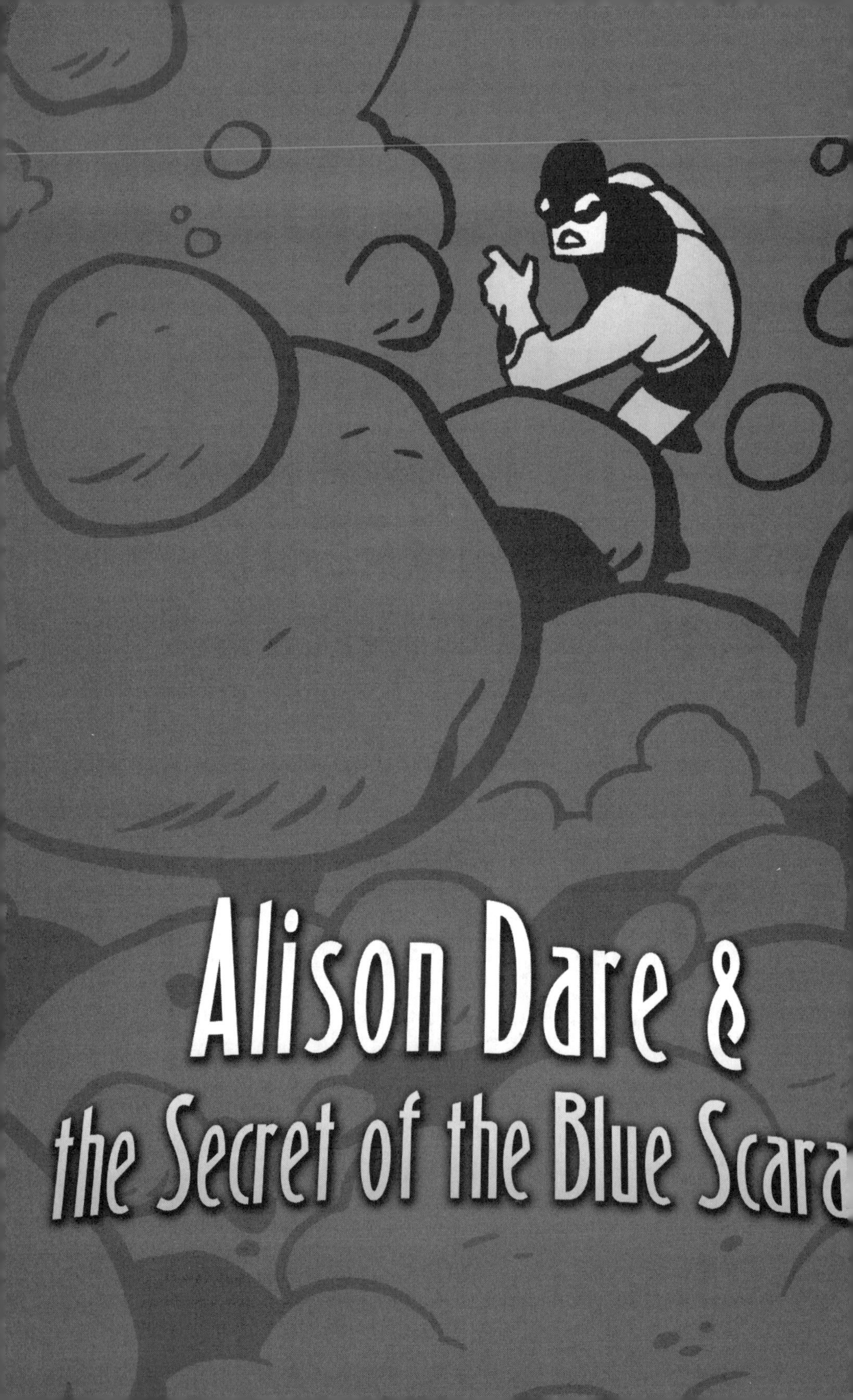

Alison Dare &
the Secret of the Blue Scara

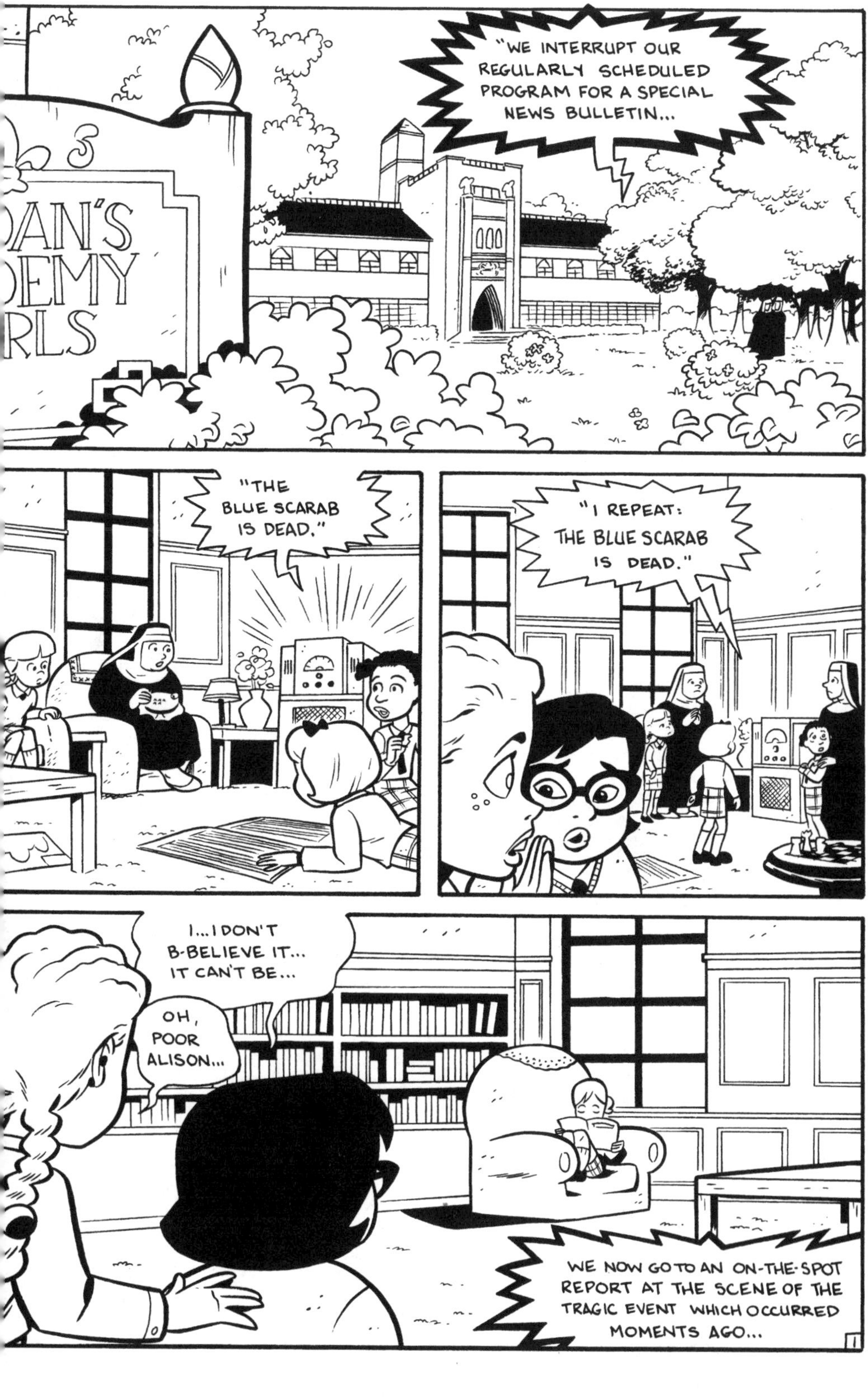
"WE INTERRUPT OUR REGULARLY SCHEDULED PROGRAM FOR A SPECIAL NEWS BULLETIN...
"THE BLUE SCARAB IS DEAD."
"I REPEAT: THE BLUE SCARAB IS DEAD."
I...I DON'T B-BELIEVE IT... IT CAN'T BE...
OH, POOR ALISON...
WE NOW GO TO AN ON-THE-SPOT REPORT AT THE SCENE OF THE TRAGIC EVENT WHICH OCCURRED MOMENTS AGO...

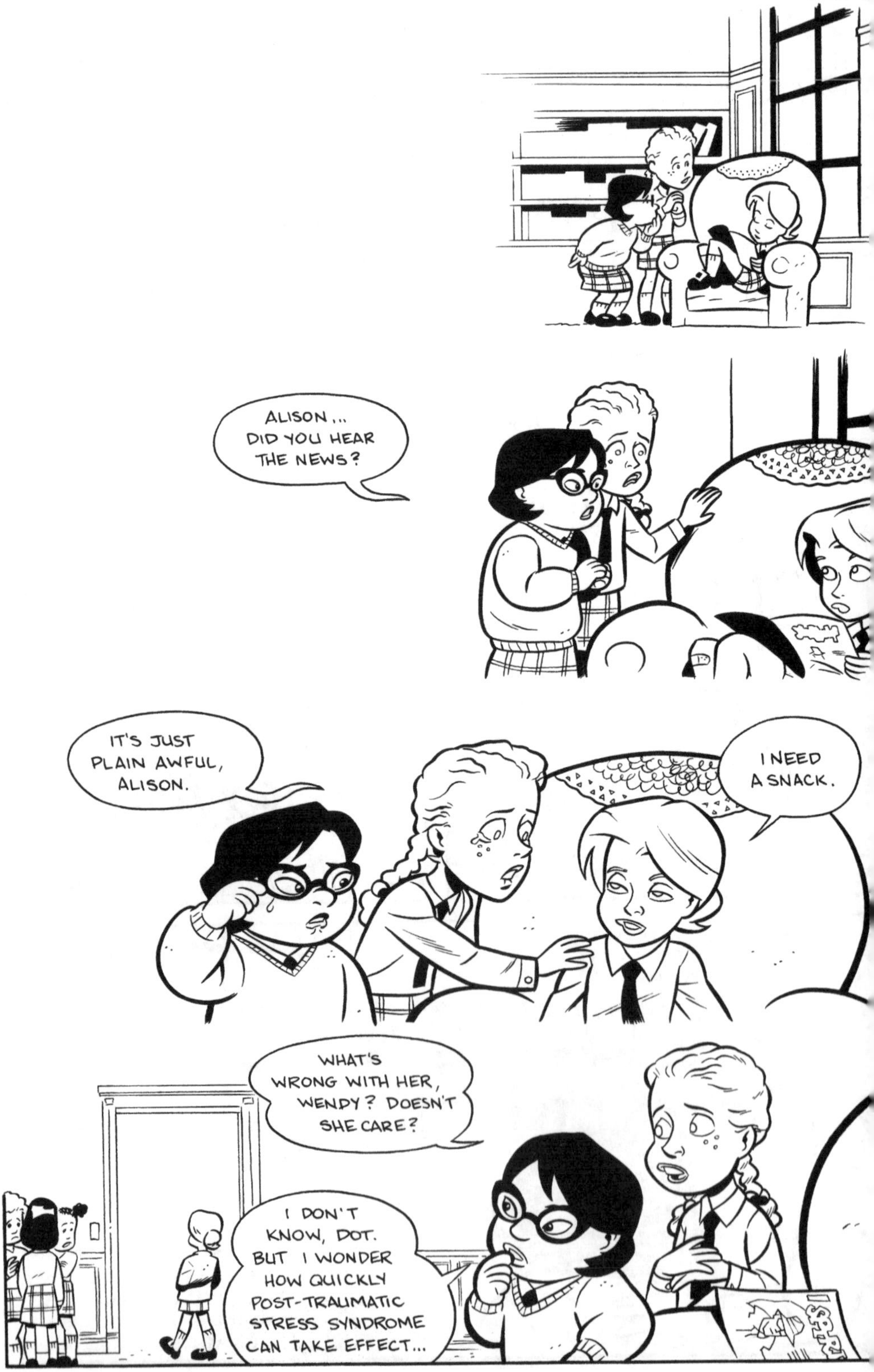
ALISON... DID YOU HEAR THE NEWS?
IT'S JUST PLAIN AWFUL, ALISON.
I NEED A SNACK.
WHAT'S WRONG WITH HER, WENDY? DOESN'T SHE CARE?
I DON'T KNOW, DOT. BUT I WONDER HOW QUICKLY POST-TRAUMATIC STRESS SYNDROME CAN TAKE EFFECT...

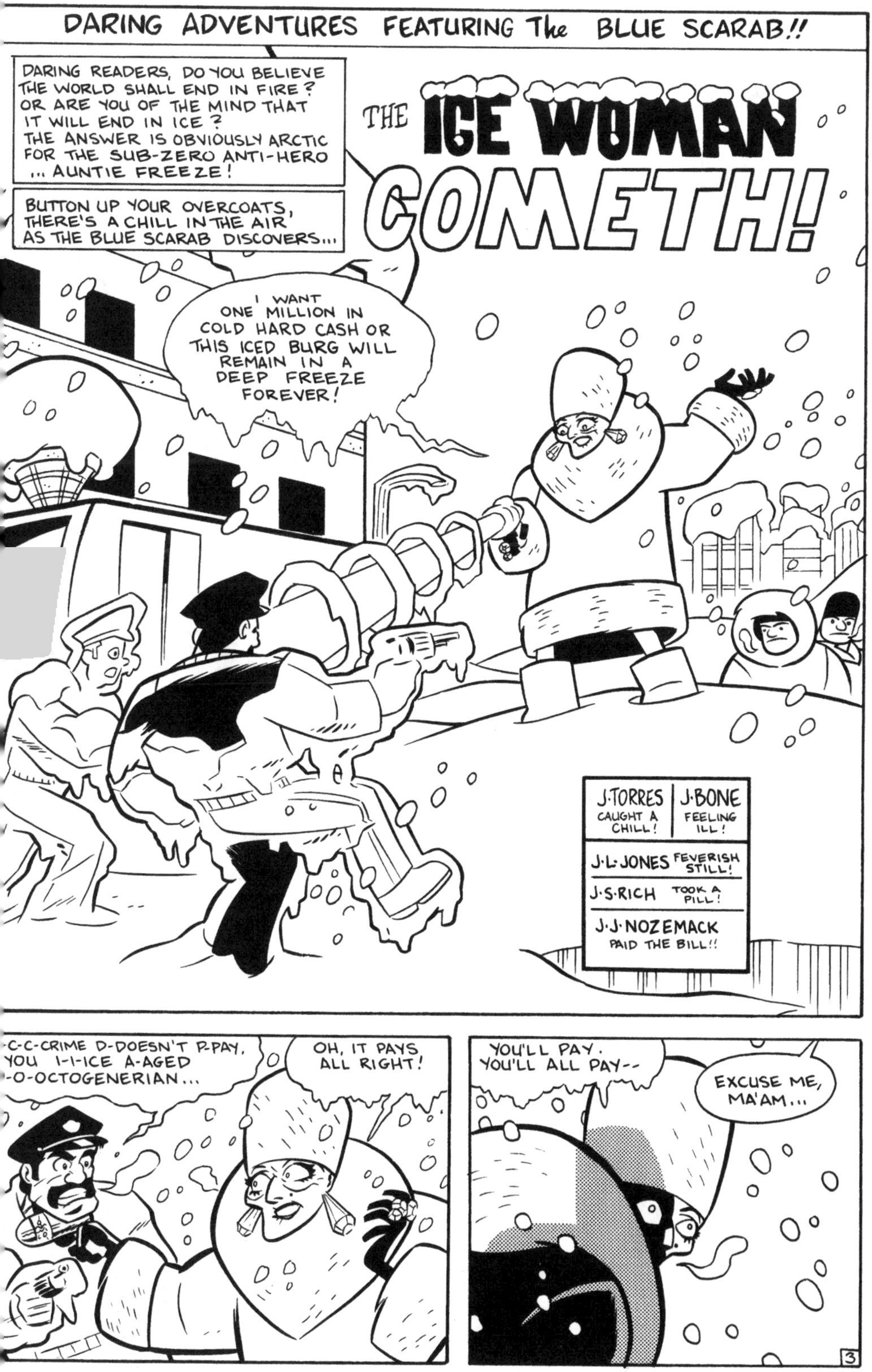

DARING ADVENTURES FEATURING The BLUE SCARAB!!
DARING READERS, DO YOU BELIEVE THE WORLD SHALL END IN FIRE? OR ARE YOU OF THE MIND THAT IT WILL END IN ICE? THE ANSWER IS OBVIOUSLY ARCTIC FOR THE SUB-ZERO ANTI-HERO ... AUNTIE FREEZE!
BUTTON UP YOUR OVERCOATS, THERE'S A CHILL IN THE AIR AS THE BLUE SCARAB DISCOVERS...
THE ICE WOMAN COMETH!
I WANT ONE MILLION IN COLD HARD CASH OR THIS ICED BURG WILL REMAIN IN A DEEP FREEZE FOREVER!
J·TORRES CAUGHT A CHILL!
J·BONE FEELING ILL!
J·L·JONES FEVERISH STILL!
J·S·RICH TOOK A PILL!
J·J·NOZEMACK PAID THE BILL!!
C-C-CRIME D-DOESN'T P-PAY, YOU I-I-ICE A-AGED -O-OCTOGENERIAN...
OH, IT PAYS ALL RIGHT!
YOU'LL PAY. YOU'LL ALL PAY--
EXCUSE ME, MA'AM...

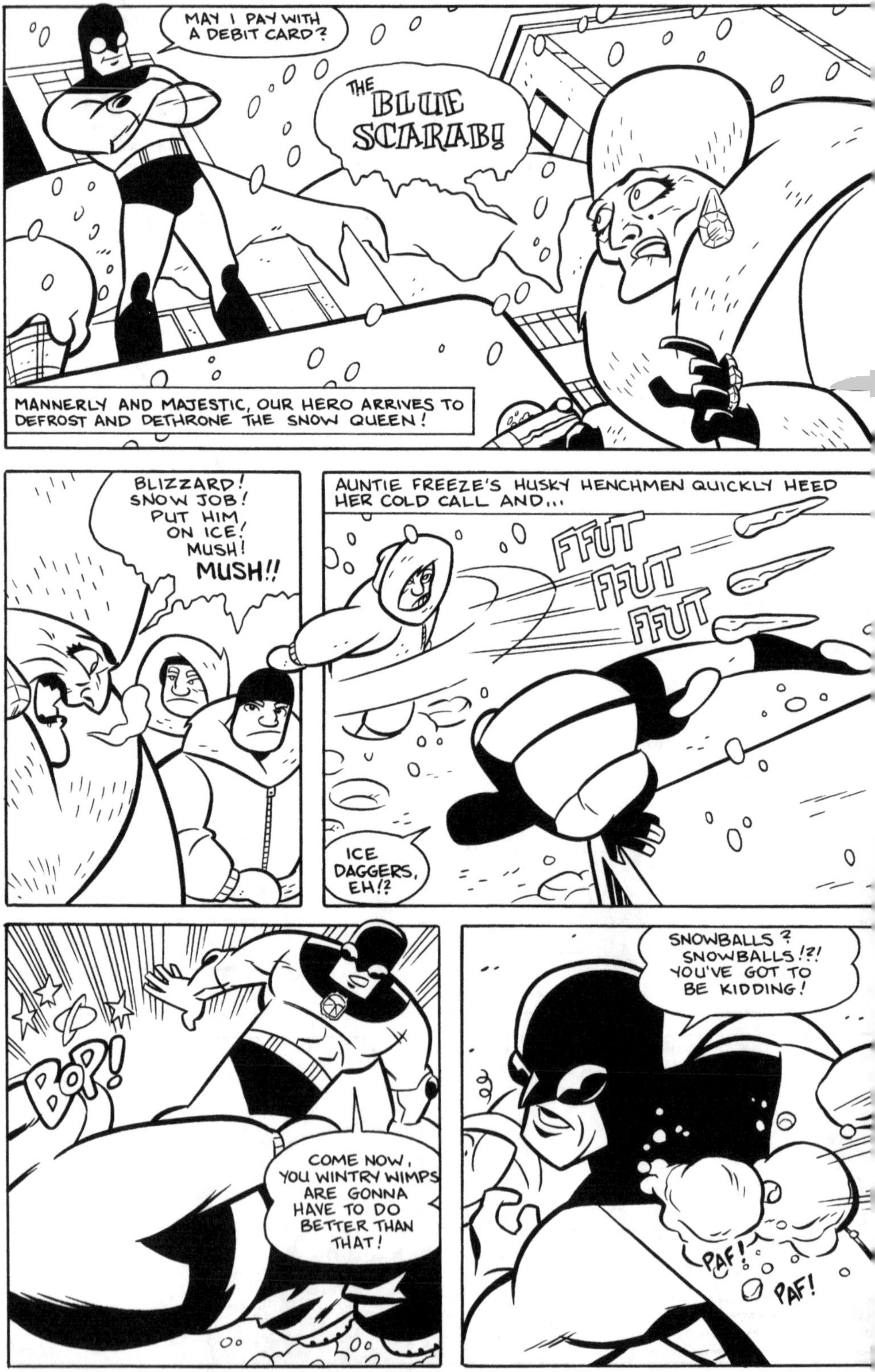
MAY I PAY WITH A DEBIT CARD?
THE BLUE SCARAB!
MANNERLY AND MAJESTIC, OUR HERO ARRIVES TO DEFROST AND DETHRONE THE SNOW QUEEN!
BLIZZARD! SNOW JOB! PUT HIM ON ICE! MUSH! MUSH!!
AUNTIE FREEZE'S HUSKY HENCHMEN QUICKLY HEED HER COLD CALL AND...
FFUT FFUT FFUT
ICE DAGGERS, EH!?
BOP!
COME NOW, YOU WINTRY WIMPS ARE GONNA HAVE TO DO BETTER THAN THAT!
SNOWBALLS? SNOWBALLS!?! YOU'VE GOT TO BE KIDDING!
PAF! PAF!

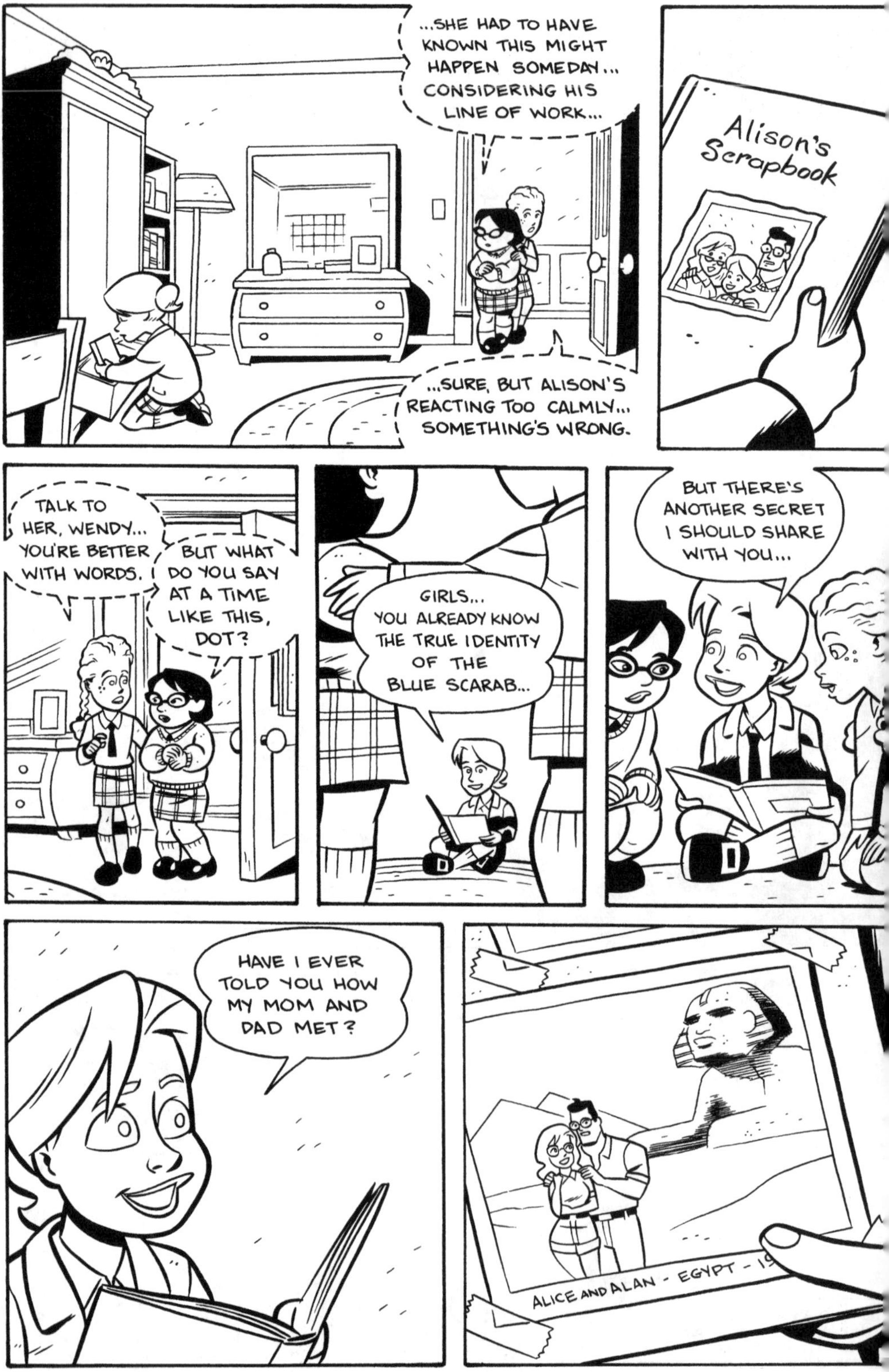
...SHE HAD TO HAVE KNOWN THIS MIGHT HAPPEN SOMEDAY... CONSIDERING HIS LINE OF WORK...
...SURE, BUT ALISON'S REACTING TOO CALMLY... SOMETHING'S WRONG.
Alison's Scrapbook
TALK TO HER, WENDY... YOU'RE BETTER WITH WORDS.
BUT WHAT DO YOU SAY AT A TIME LIKE THIS, DOT?
GIRLS... YOU ALREADY KNOW THE TRUE IDENTITY OF THE BLUE SCARAB...
BUT THERE'S ANOTHER SECRET I SHOULD SHARE WITH YOU...
HAVE I EVER TOLD YOU HOW MY MOM AND DAD MET?
ALICE AND ALAN - EGYPT - 19

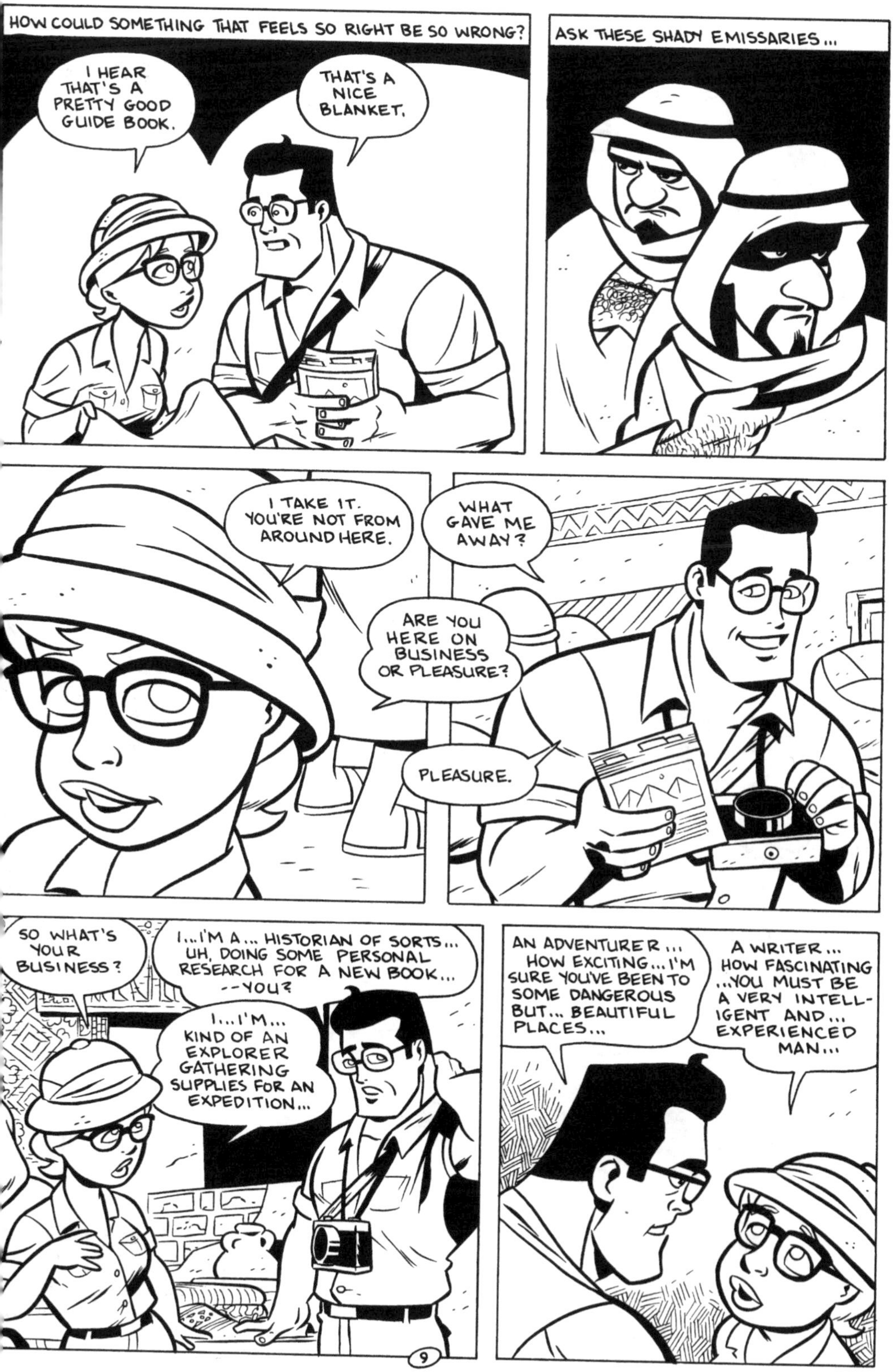
HOW COULD SOMETHING THAT FEELS SO RIGHT BE SO WRONG?
I HEAR THAT'S A PRETTY GOOD GUIDE BOOK.
THAT'S A NICE BLANKET.
ASK THESE SHADY EMISSARIES...
I TAKE IT. YOU'RE NOT FROM AROUND HERE.
WHAT GAVE ME AWAY?
ARE YOU HERE ON BUSINESS OR PLEASURE?
PLEASURE.
SO WHAT'S YOUR BUSINESS?
I...I'M A... HISTORIAN OF SORTS... UH, DOING SOME PERSONAL RESEARCH FOR A NEW BOOK... --YOU?
I...I'M... KIND OF AN EXPLORER GATHERING SUPPLIES FOR AN EXPEDITION...
AN ADVENTURER... HOW EXCITING... I'M SURE YOU'VE BEEN TO SOME DANGEROUS BUT... BEAUTIFUL PLACES...
A WRITER... HOW FASCINATING ...YOU MUST BE A VERY INTELLIGENT AND... EXPERIENCED MAN...

SUDDENLY, A BEAUTIFUL MOMENT...

TURNS UGLY...

MISS DARE, WE HAVE AN IMPORTANT MESSAGE FOR YOU.

WHAT IS THIS?

IT'S NO LOVE LETTER!

GASP!

IS EVERYTHING ALL RIGHT?

BUT SOMETIMES EVEN WHEN LOVE IS ILL-FATED IT MUST STILL COME TO PASS...

COME WITH US.

S-SORRY... I HAVE TO GO...

MISS DARE IF YOU WANT TO SEE YOUR FATHER

AFTER ALL, 'TIS BETTER TO HAVE LOVED AND LOST THAN NOT TO HAVE LOVED AT ALL...

EVEN IF THAT LOVE IS CATALYZED BY ... DANGER!

10

TO BE CONTINUED IN THE NEXT ISSUE OF

Daring Romance

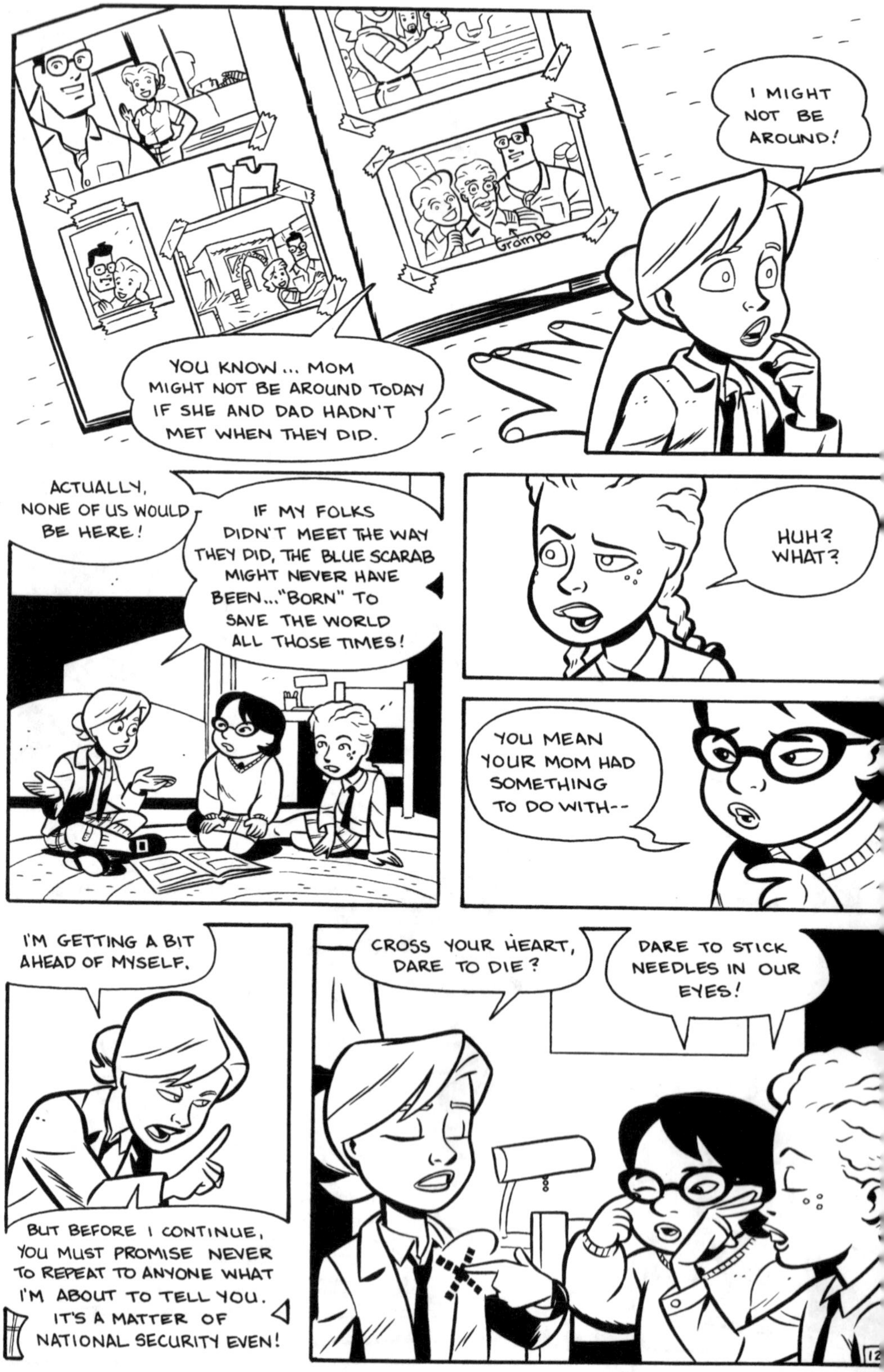

I MIGHT NOT BE AROUND!
YOU KNOW... MOM MIGHT NOT BE AROUND TODAY IF SHE AND DAD HADN'T MET WHEN THEY DID.
Grampa
ACTUALLY, NONE OF US WOULD BE HERE!
IF MY FOLKS DIDN'T MEET THE WAY THEY DID, THE BLUE SCARAB MIGHT NEVER HAVE BEEN..."BORN" TO SAVE THE WORLD ALL THOSE TIMES!
HUH? WHAT?
YOU MEAN YOUR MOM HAD SOMETHING TO DO WITH--
I'M GETTING A BIT AHEAD OF MYSELF.
BUT BEFORE I CONTINUE, YOU MUST PROMISE NEVER TO REPEAT TO ANYONE WHAT I'M ABOUT TO TELL YOU. IT'S A MATTER OF NATIONAL SECURITY EVEN!
CROSS YOUR HEART, DARE TO DIE?
DARE TO STICK NEEDLES IN OUR EYES!

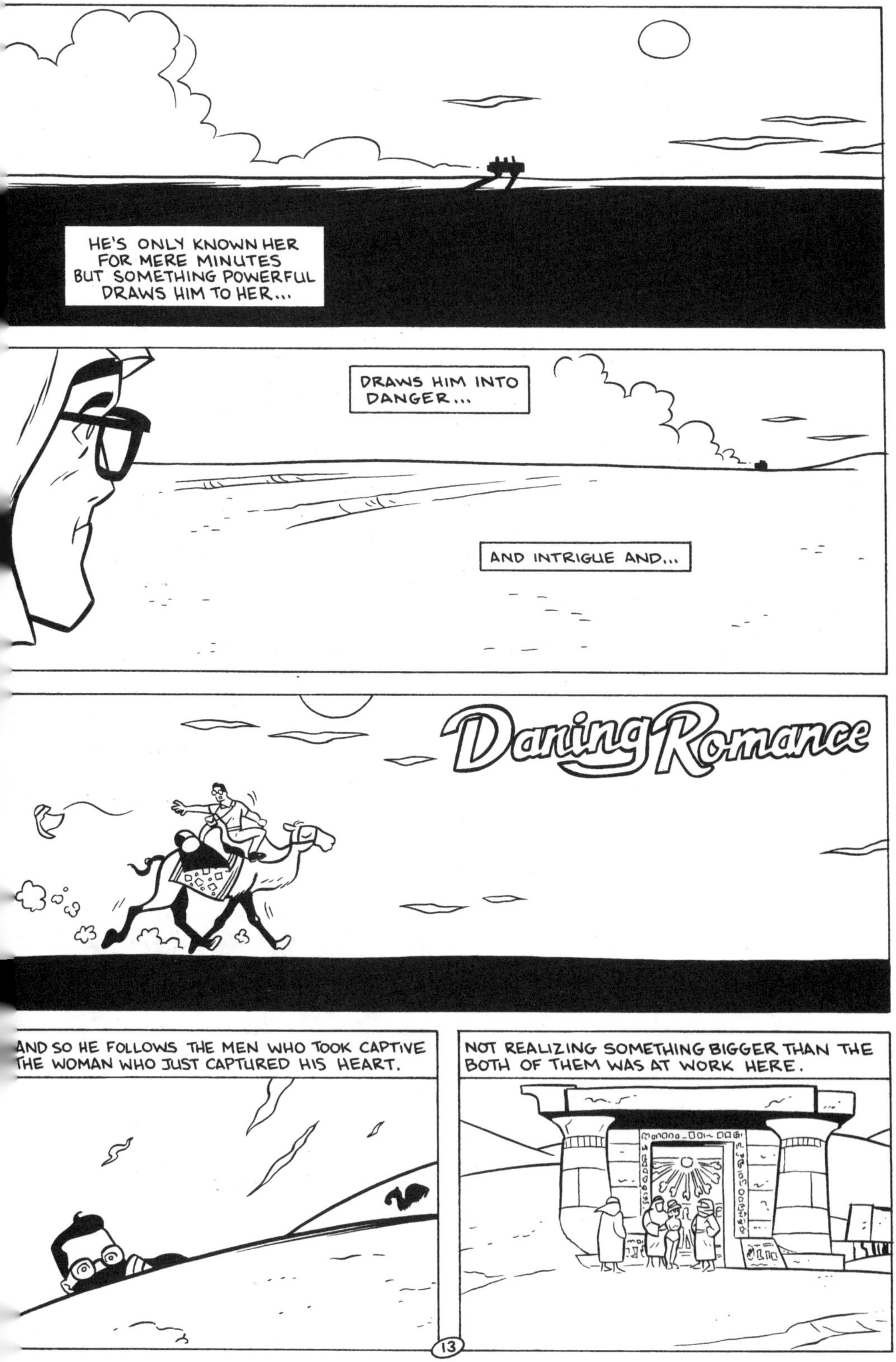
HE'S ONLY KNOWN HER FOR MERE MINUTES BUT SOMETHING POWERFUL DRAWS HIM TO HER...
DRAWS HIM INTO DANGER...
AND INTRIGUE AND...
Daring Romance
AND SO HE FOLLOWS THE MEN WHO TOOK CAPTIVE THE WOMAN WHO JUST CAPTURED HIS HEART.
NOT REALIZING SOMETHING BIGGER THAN THE BOTH OF THEM WAS AT WORK HERE.

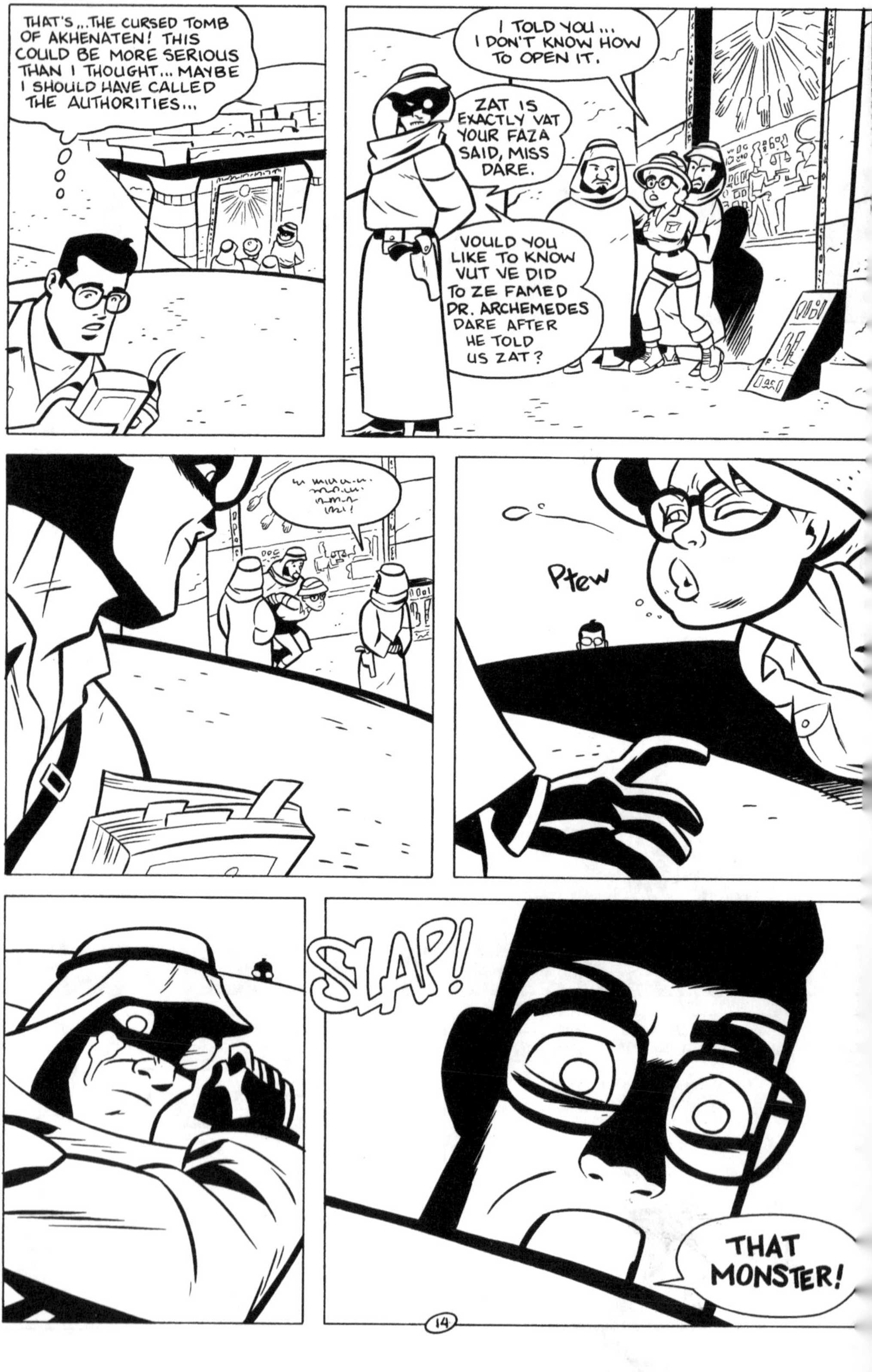
THAT'S... THE CURSED TOMB OF AKHENATEN! THIS COULD BE MORE SERIOUS THAN I THOUGHT... MAYBE I SHOULD HAVE CALLED THE AUTHORITIES...
I TOLD YOU... I DON'T KNOW HOW TO OPEN IT.
ZAT IS EXACTLY VAT YOUR FAZA SAID, MISS DARE.
VOULD YOU LIKE TO KNOW VUT VE DID TO ZE FAMED DR. ARCHEMEDES DARE AFTER HE TOLD US ZAT?
Ptew
SLAP!
THAT MONSTER!

AM NOT ROM ZE VEST. UND I SUGGEST YOU HURRY, MISS DARE, YOUR FAZA DOES NOT HAVE MUCH TIME LEFT

STOP!

PROMISE NOT TO HARM HER AND I'LL GO...

WHAT AM I LOOKING FOR?

YOU ARE LOOKINK FOR ZIS: ZE AMULET OF ZE BLUE SCARAB. IT IS SAID TO CONTAIN ZE POWER OF ZE GODS ZEMSELVES.

NO...PLEASE... THE CURSE... LET ME GO IN...

THINK OF YOUR FATHER...IF ANYTHING SHOULD HAPPEN TO YOU WHO'LL SAVE HIM?

I-I DON'T EVEN KNOW YOUR NAME.

IT'S ALAN. ALAN DODD. AND I LIED ABOUT BEING A "HISTORIAN"... I'M JUST A LIBRARIAN ON HOLIDAY...

MY NAME IS ALICE...AND I'M JUST AN ARCHAEOLOGY STUDENT TAGGING ALONG WITH HER FAMOUS FATHER ON AN EXCAVATION...

ENOUGH VIS ZE CONFESSIONS!

TAKE ZIS UND GO GET ZE AMULET, "SUPERHERO"...

AND SO, THE LIBRARIAN ENTERS THE UNKNOWN, UNSURE IF HE'LL EVER SEE HIS NEW LOVE'S FACE EVER AGAIN...

...AND YET KNOWING SHOULD HE PERISH SO THAT SHE MAY LIVE, IT WOULD BE WORTH THE FLEETING TIME THEY SHARED!

17

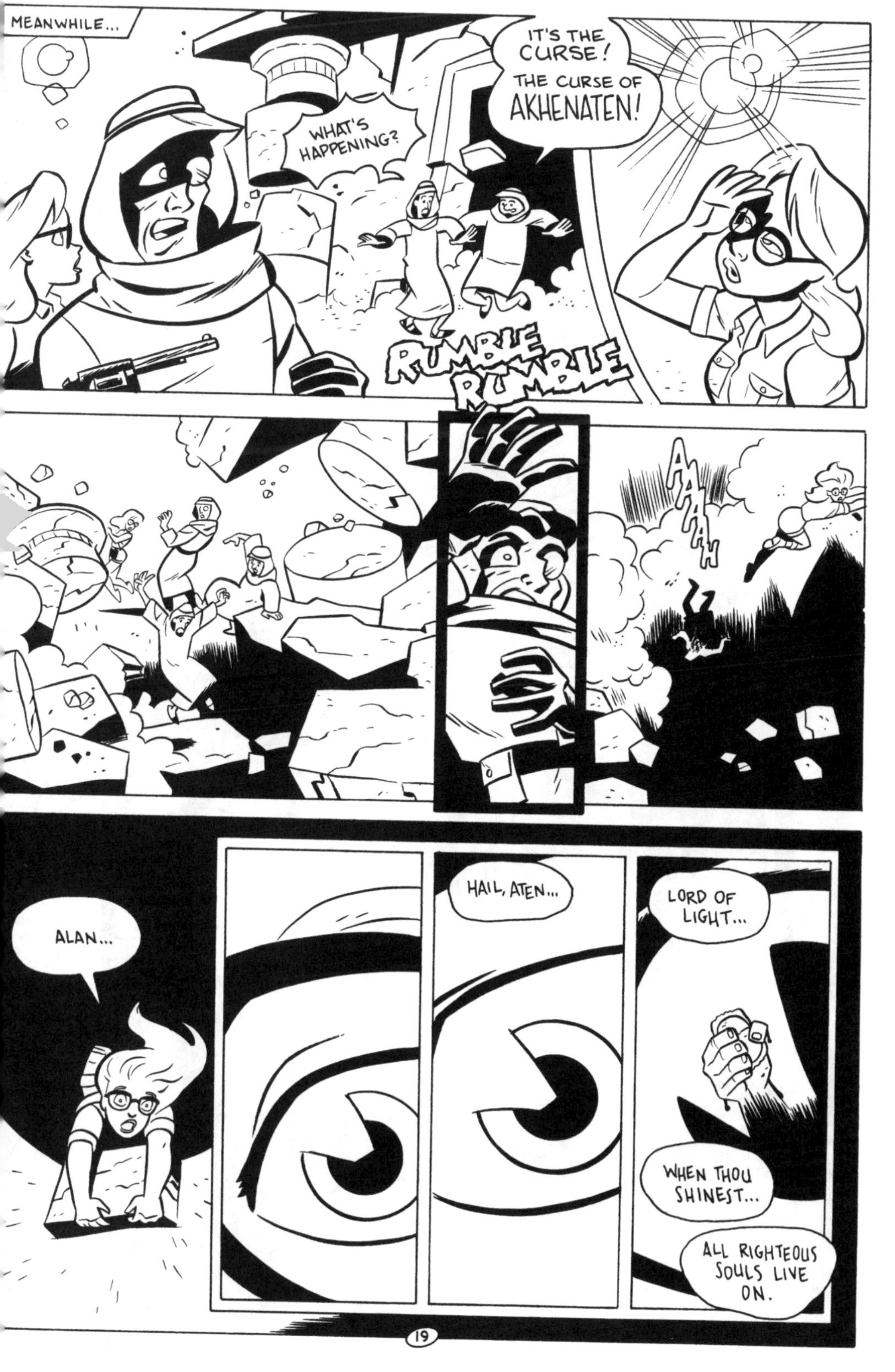
MEANWHILE...
WHAT'S HAPPENING?
IT'S THE CURSE!
THE CURSE OF AKHENATEN!
RUMBLE RUMBLE
AAAAH
ALAN...
HAIL, ATEN...
LORD OF LIGHT...
WHEN THOU SHINEST...
ALL RIGHTEOUS SOULS LIVE ON.

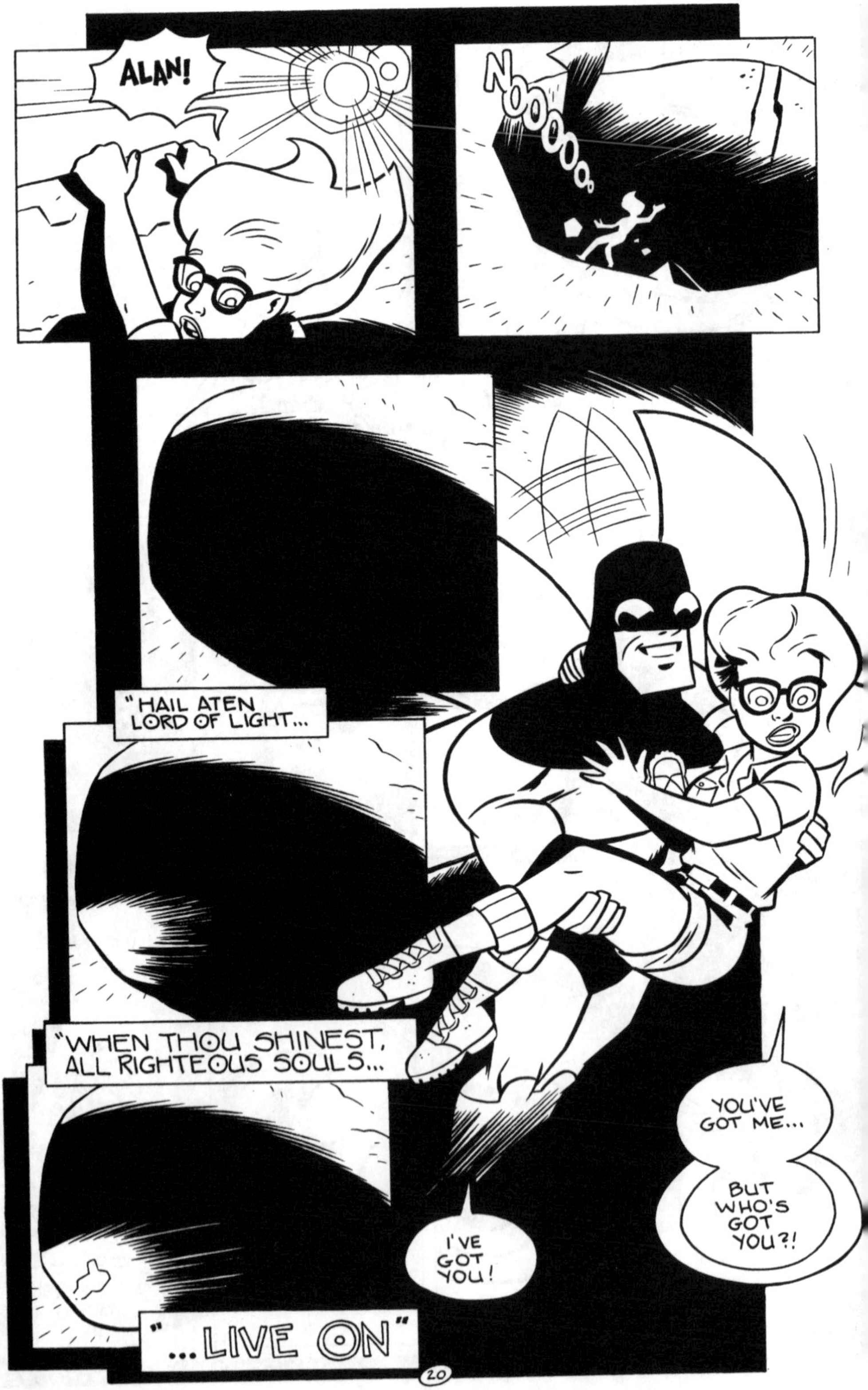
ALAN!
NOOOOOo
"HAIL ATEN
LORD OF LIGHT...
"WHEN THOU SHINEST,
ALL RIGHTEOUS SOULS...
"...LIVE ON"
I'VE GOT YOU!
YOU'VE GOT ME...
BUT WHO'S GOT YOU?!

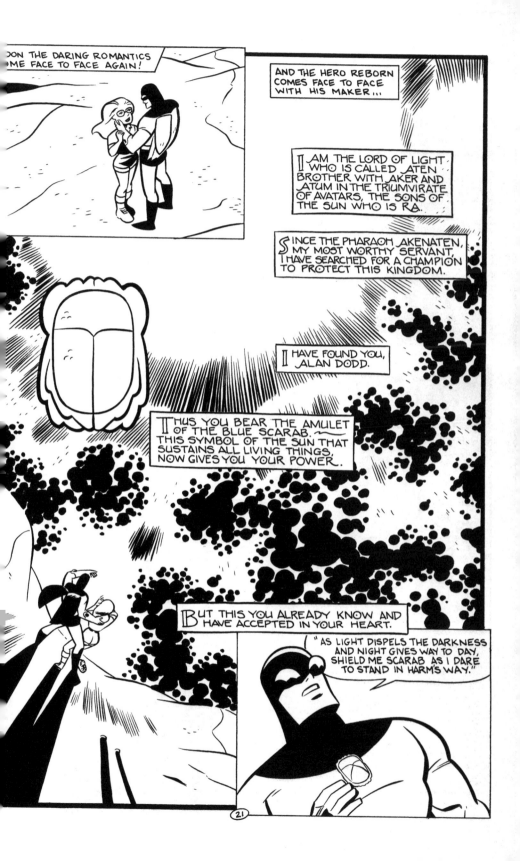

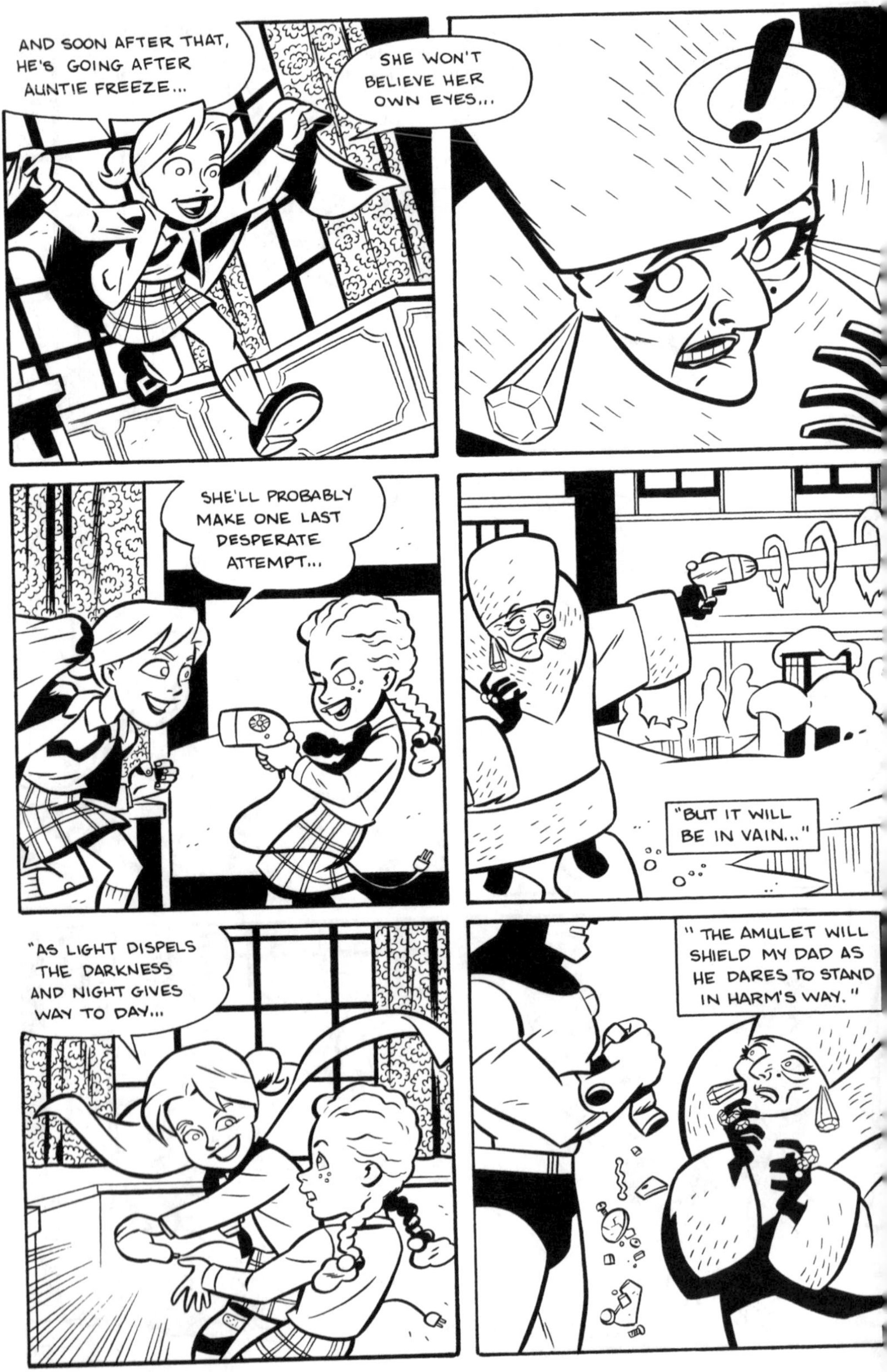
AND SOON AFTER THAT, HE'S GOING AFTER AUNTIE FREEZE...
SHE WON'T BELIEVE HER OWN EYES...
!
SHE'LL PROBABLY MAKE ONE LAST DESPERATE ATTEMPT...
"BUT IT WILL BE IN VAIN..."
"AS LIGHT DISPELS THE DARKNESS AND NIGHT GIVES WAY TO DAY...
" THE AMULET WILL SHIELD MY DAD AS HE DARES TO STAND IN HARM'S WAY."

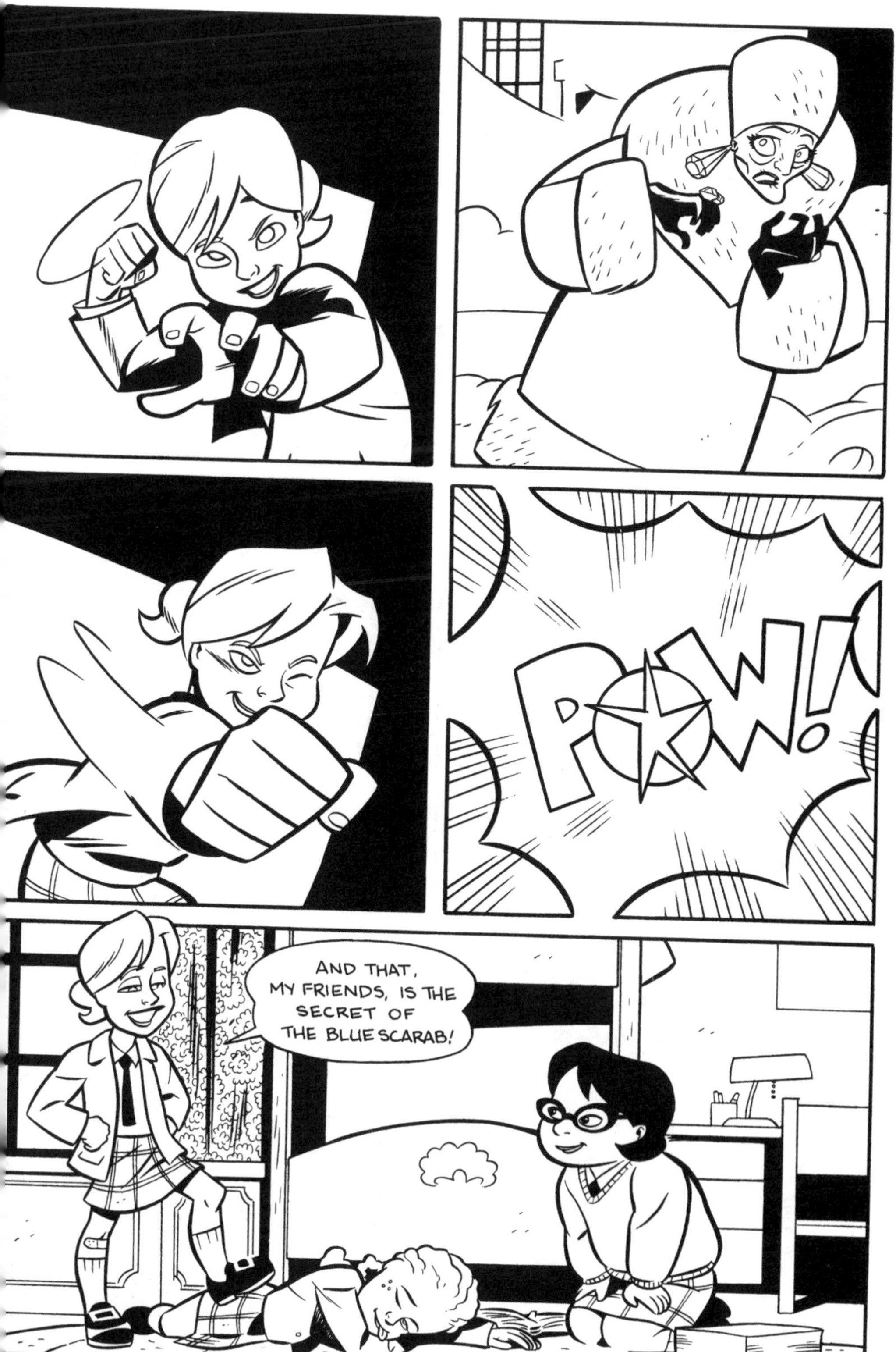
POW!
AND THAT, MY FRIENDS, IS THE SECRET OF THE BLUE SCARAB!

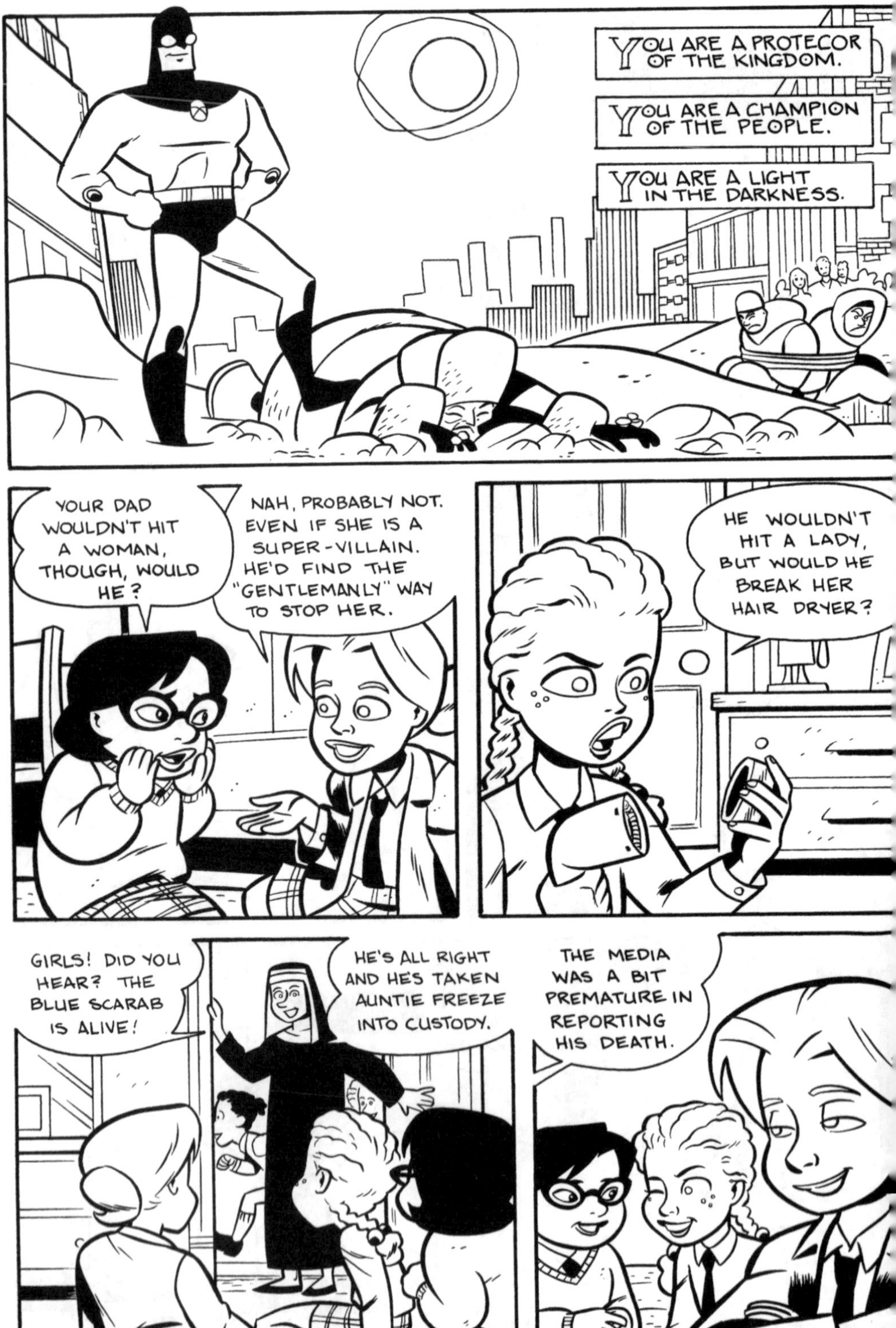
YOU ARE A PROTECOR OF THE KINGDOM.
YOU ARE A CHAMPION OF THE PEOPLE.
YOU ARE A LIGHT IN THE DARKNESS.
YOUR DAD WOULDN'T HIT A WOMAN, THOUGH, WOULD HE?
NAH, PROBABLY NOT. EVEN IF SHE IS A SUPER-VILLAIN. HE'D FIND THE "GENTLEMANLY" WAY TO STOP HER.
HE WOULDN'T HIT A LADY, BUT WOULD HE BREAK HER HAIR DRYER?
GIRLS! DID YOU HEAR? THE BLUE SCARAB IS ALIVE!
HE'S ALL RIGHT AND HE'S TAKEN AUNTIE FREEZE INTO CUSTODY.
THE MEDIA WAS A BIT PREMATURE IN REPORTING HIS DEATH.

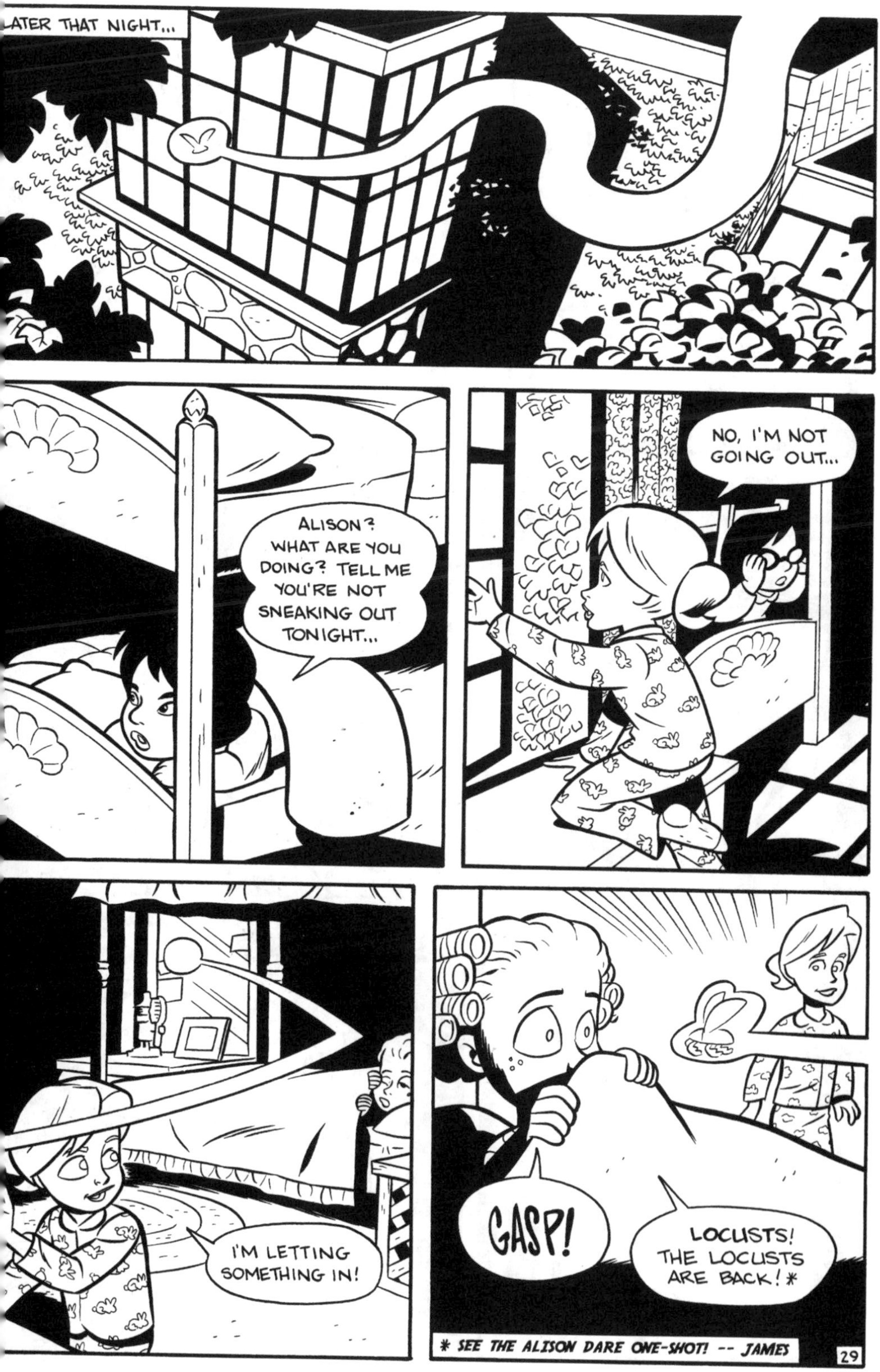
LATER THAT NIGHT...
ALISON? WHAT ARE YOU DOING? TELL ME YOU'RE NOT SNEAKING OUT TONIGHT...
NO, I'M NOT GOING OUT...
I'M LETTING SOMETHING IN!
GASP!
LOCUSTS! THE LOCUSTS ARE BACK! *
* SEE THE ALISON DARE ONE-SHOT! -- JAMES

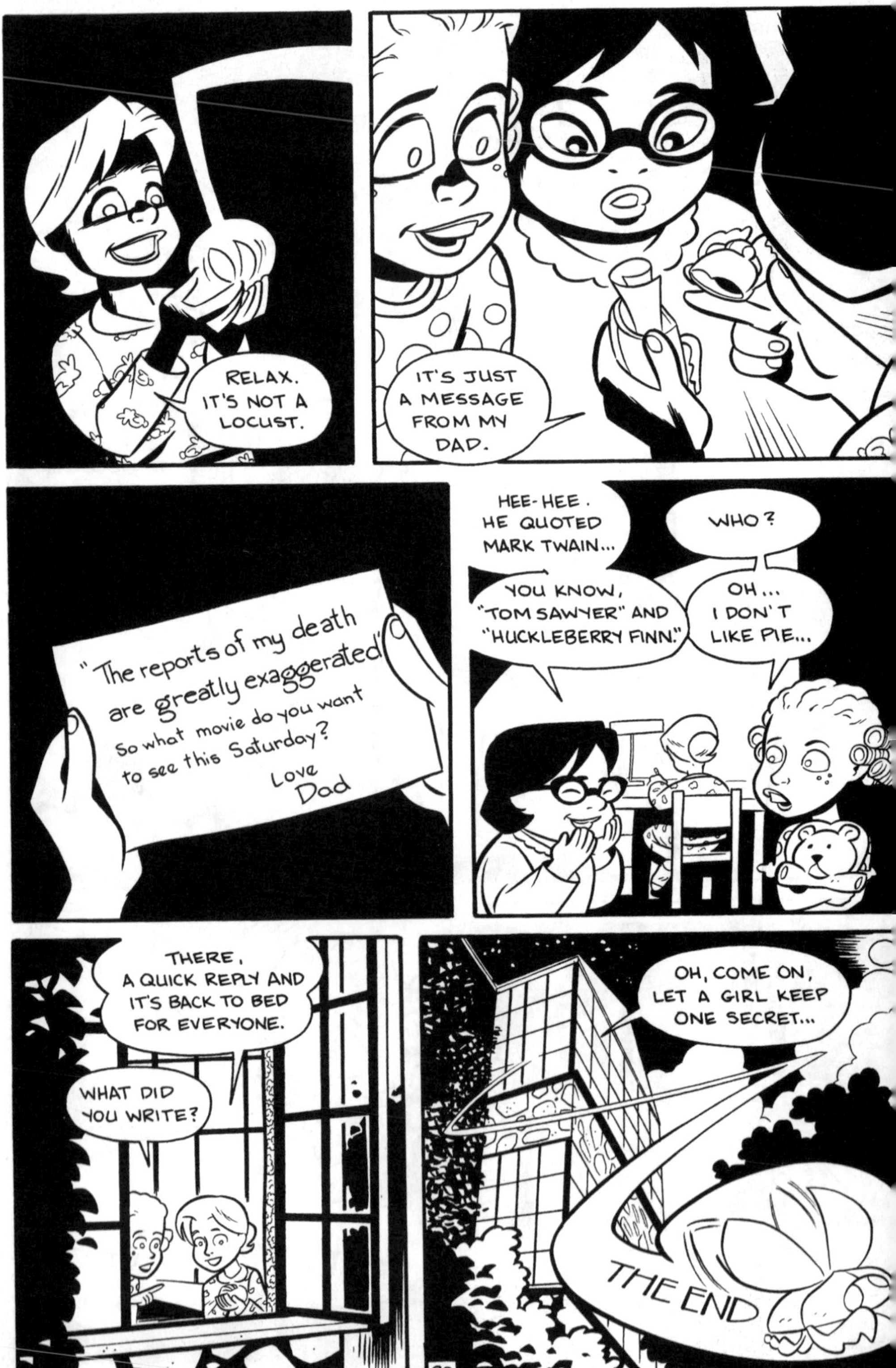
RELAX. IT'S NOT A LOCUST.
IT'S JUST A MESSAGE FROM MY DAD.
"The reports of my death are greatly exaggerated" So what movie do you want to see this Saturday? Love Dad
HEE-HEE. HE QUOTED MARK TWAIN...
WHO?
YOU KNOW, "TOM SAWYER" AND "HUCKLEBERRY FINN."
OH... I DON'T LIKE PIE...
THERE, A QUICK REPLY AND IT'S BACK TO BED FOR EVERYONE.
WHAT DID YOU WRITE?
OH, COME ON, LET A GIRL KEEP ONE SECRET...
THE END
30

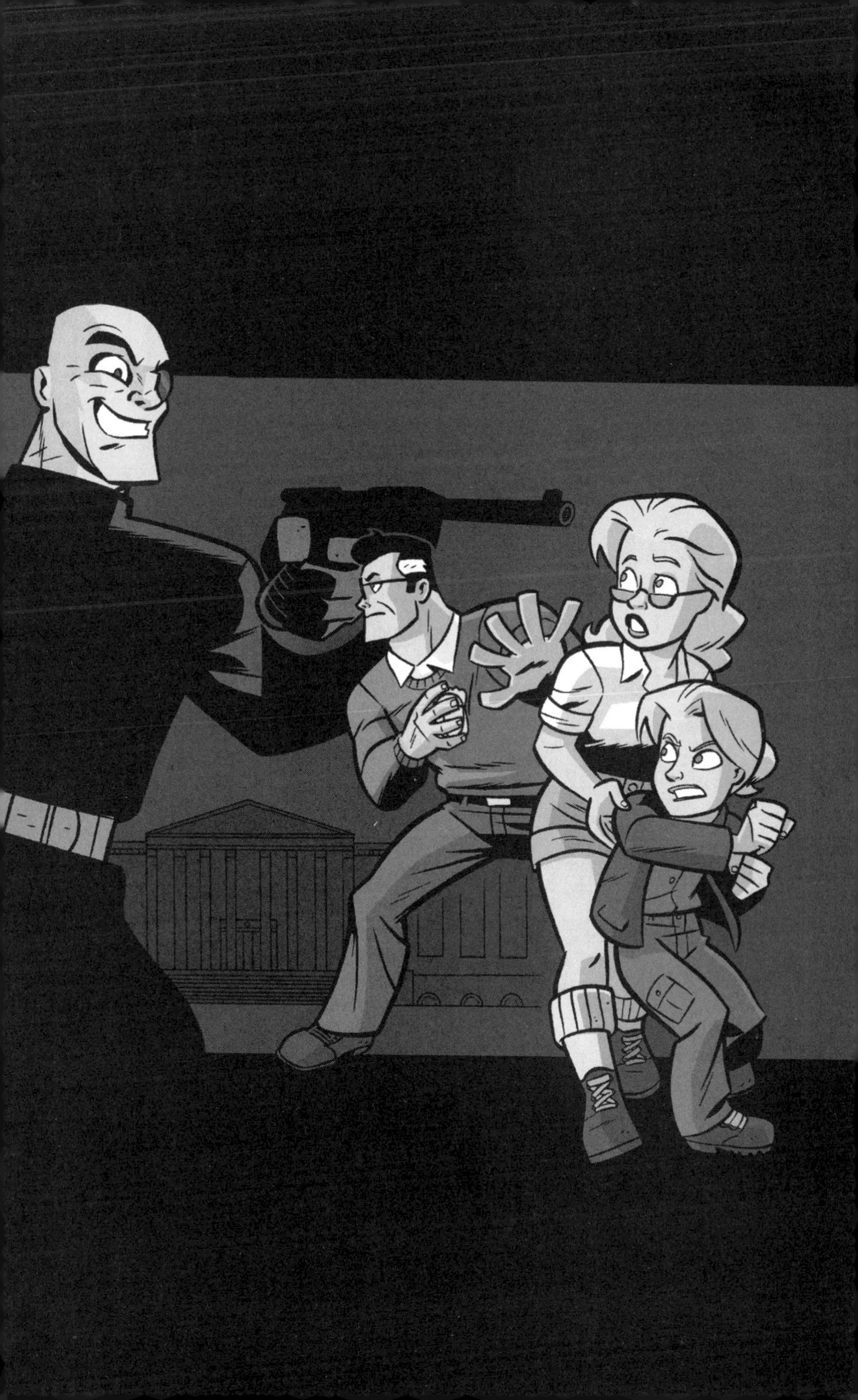

Alison Dare & the Mummy Child

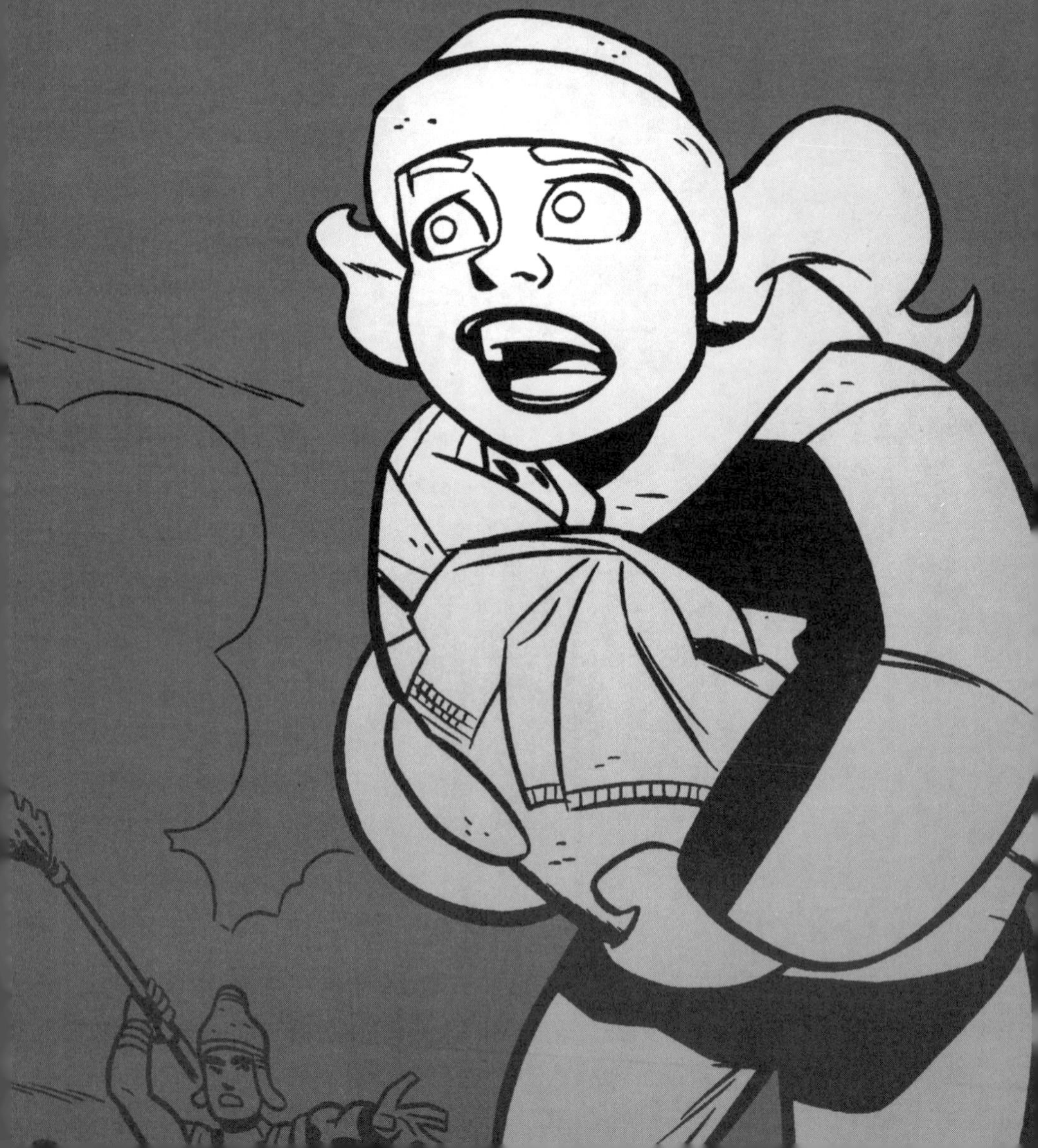

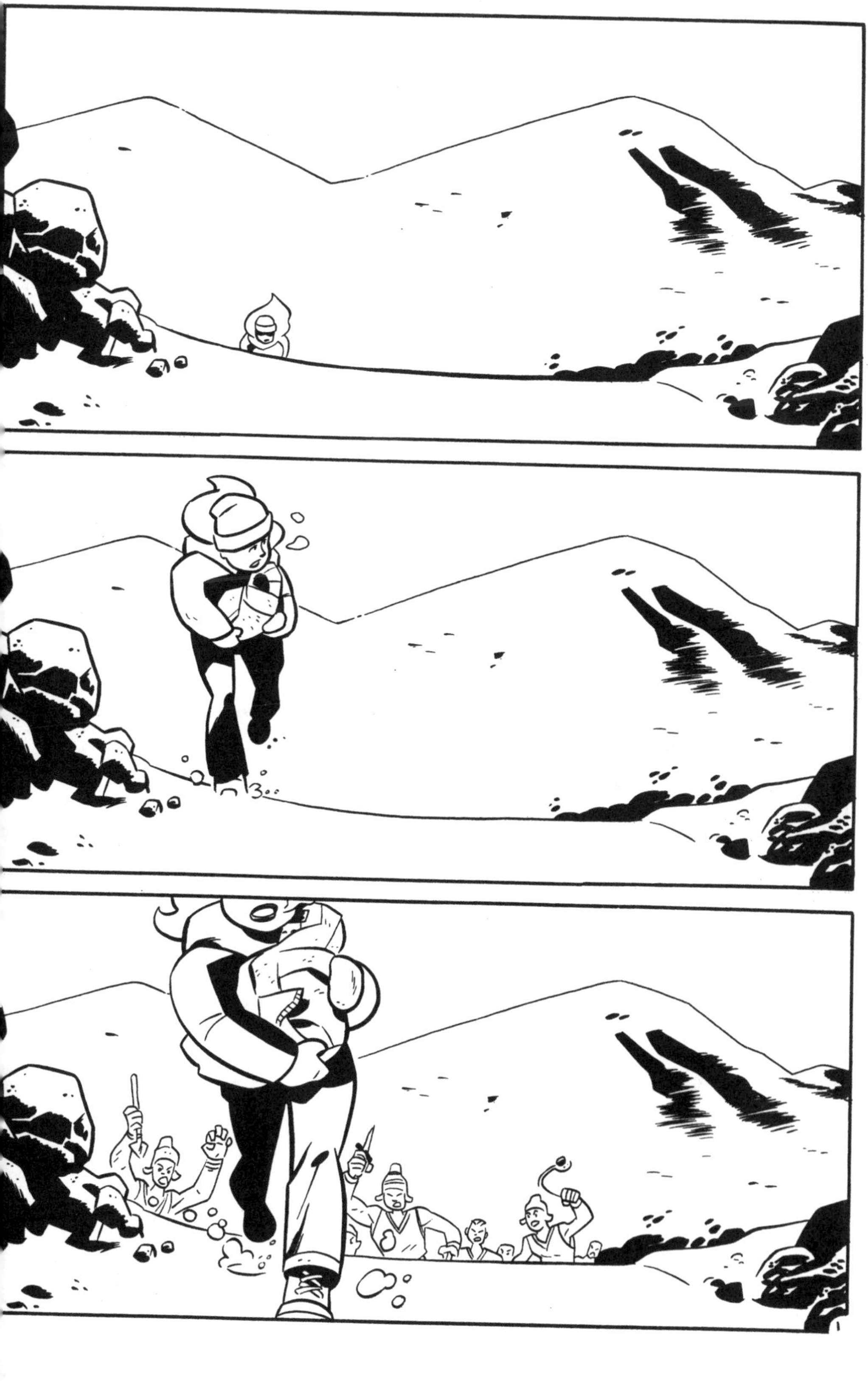

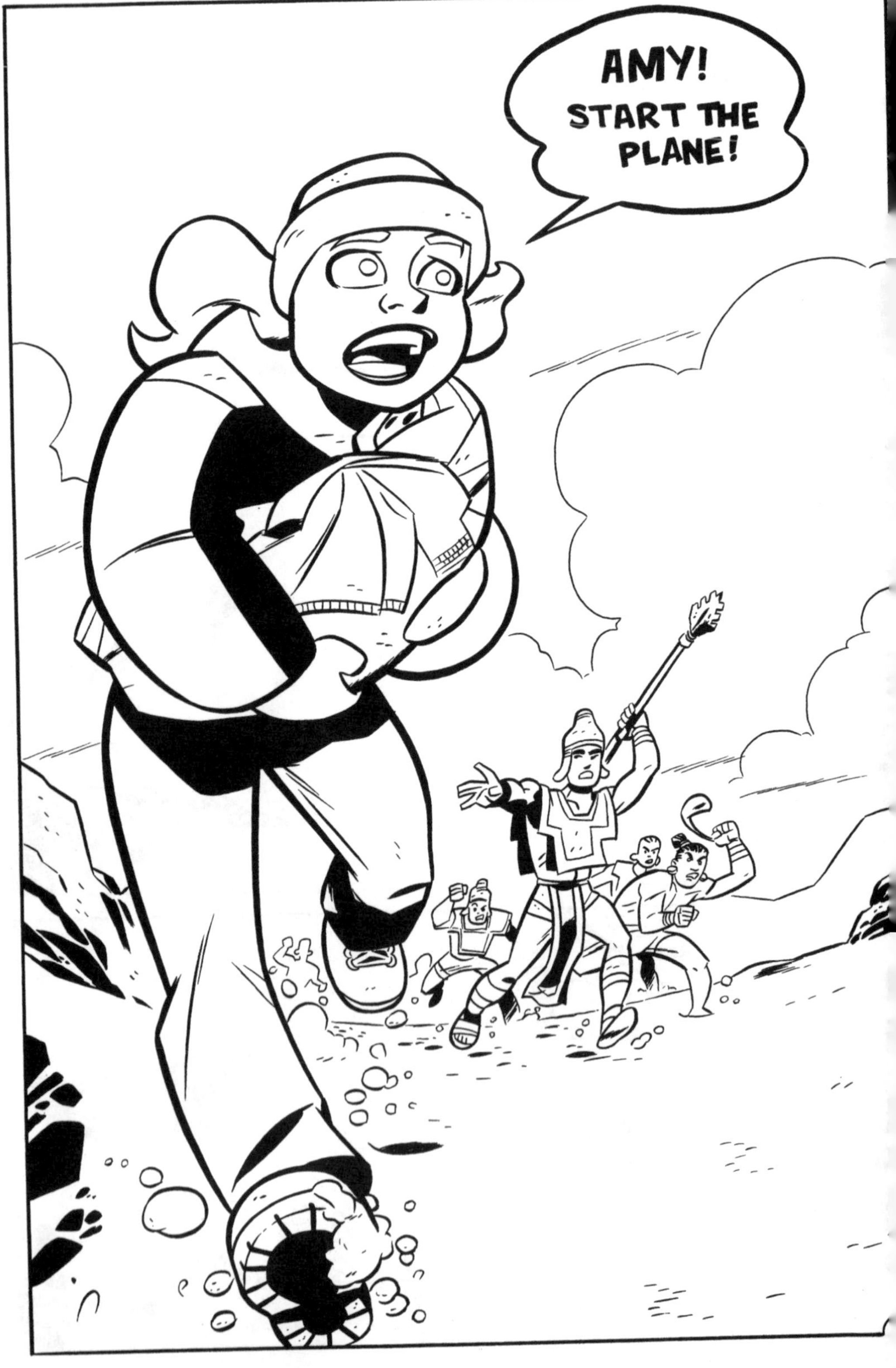
AMY! START THE PLANE!

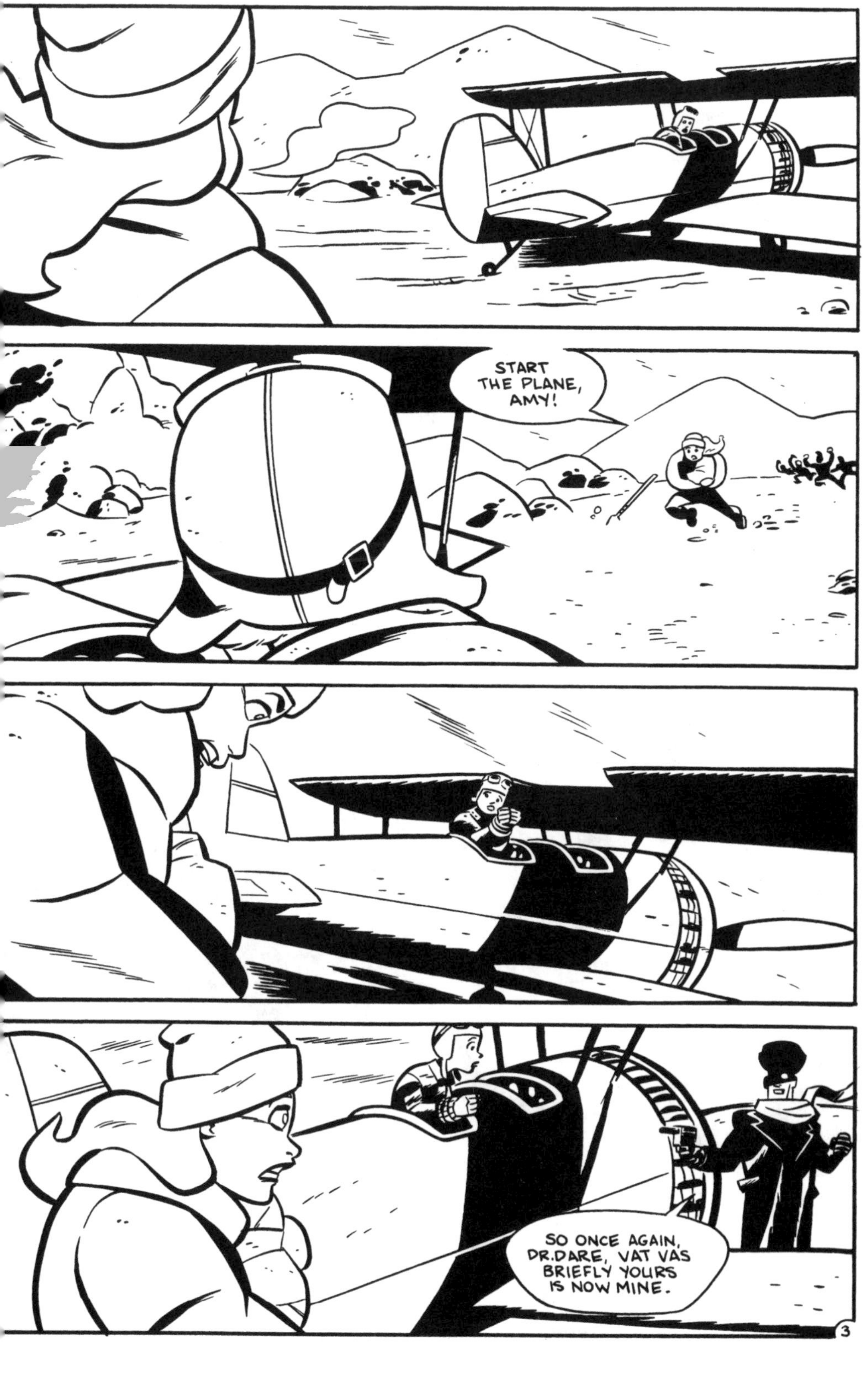
START THE PLANE, AMY!
SO ONCE AGAIN, DR.DARE, VAT VAS BRIEFLY YOURS IS NOW MINE.

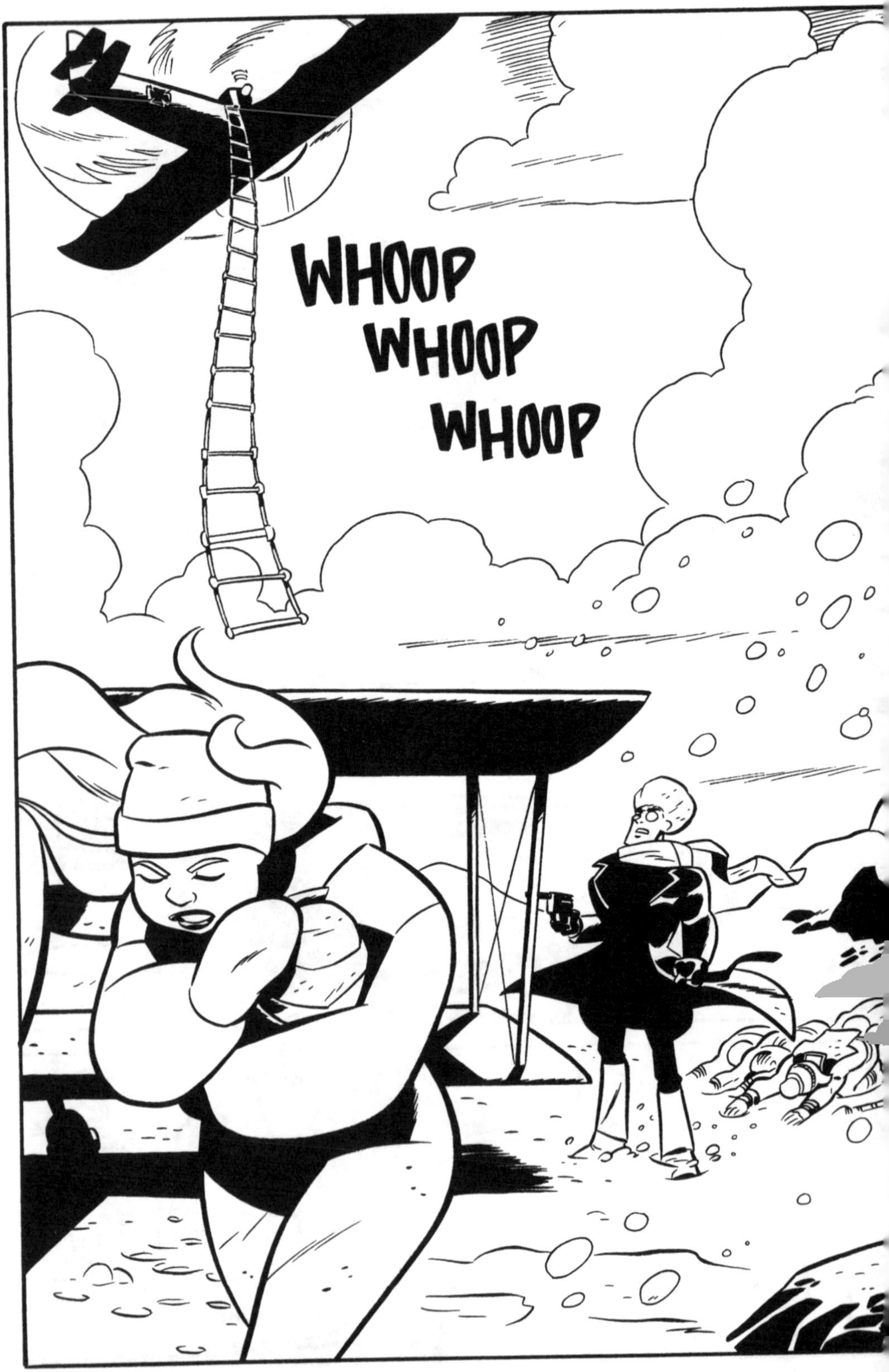
WHOOP
WHOOP
WHOOP

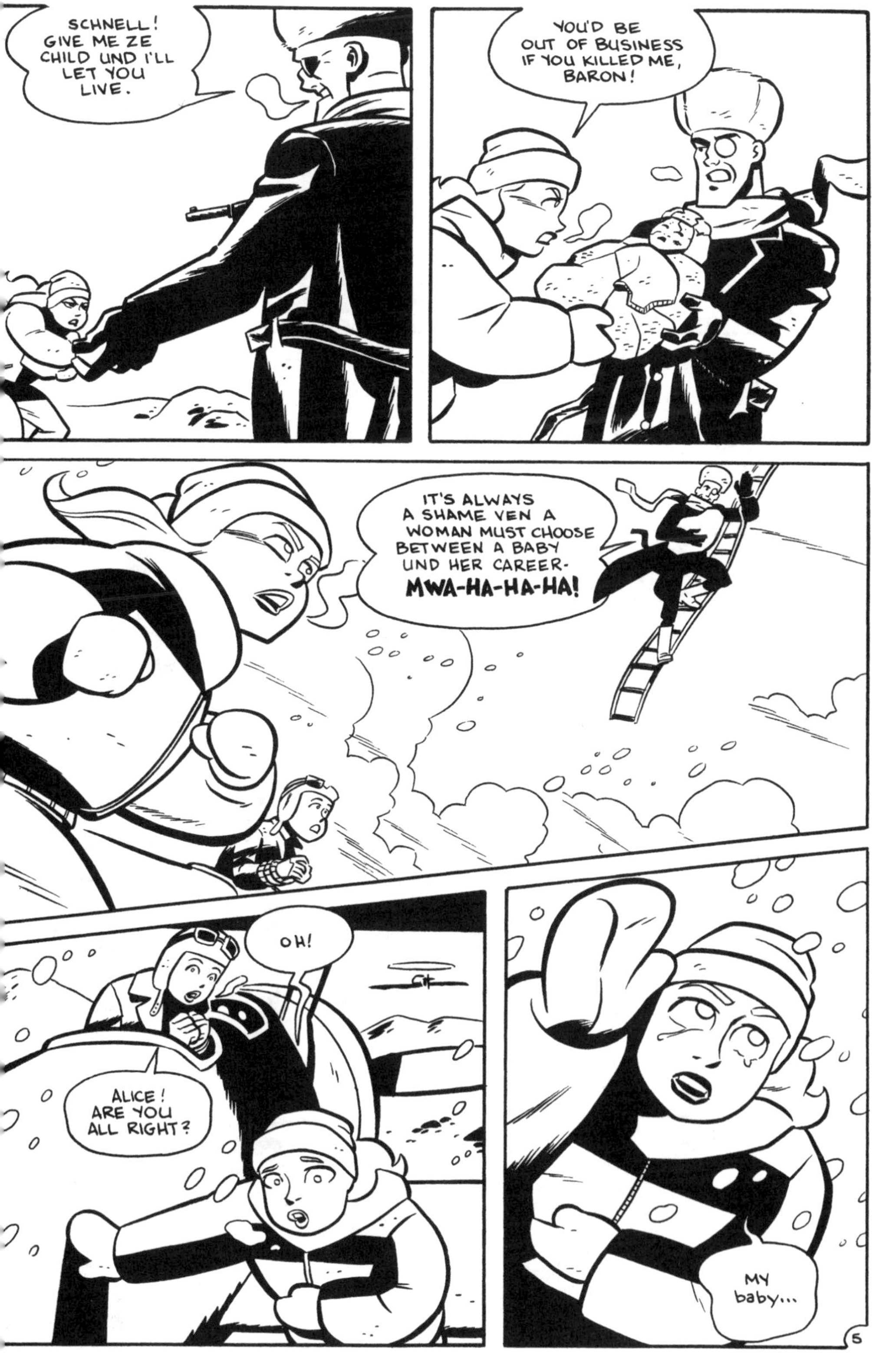
SCHNELL! GIVE ME ZE CHILD UND I'LL LET YOU LIVE.
YOU'D BE OUT OF BUSINESS IF YOU KILLED ME, BARON!
IT'S ALWAYS A SHAME VEN A WOMAN MUST CHOOSE BETWEEN A BABY UND HER CAREER- MWA-HA-HA-HA!
OH!
ALICE! ARE YOU ALL RIGHT?
MY baby...

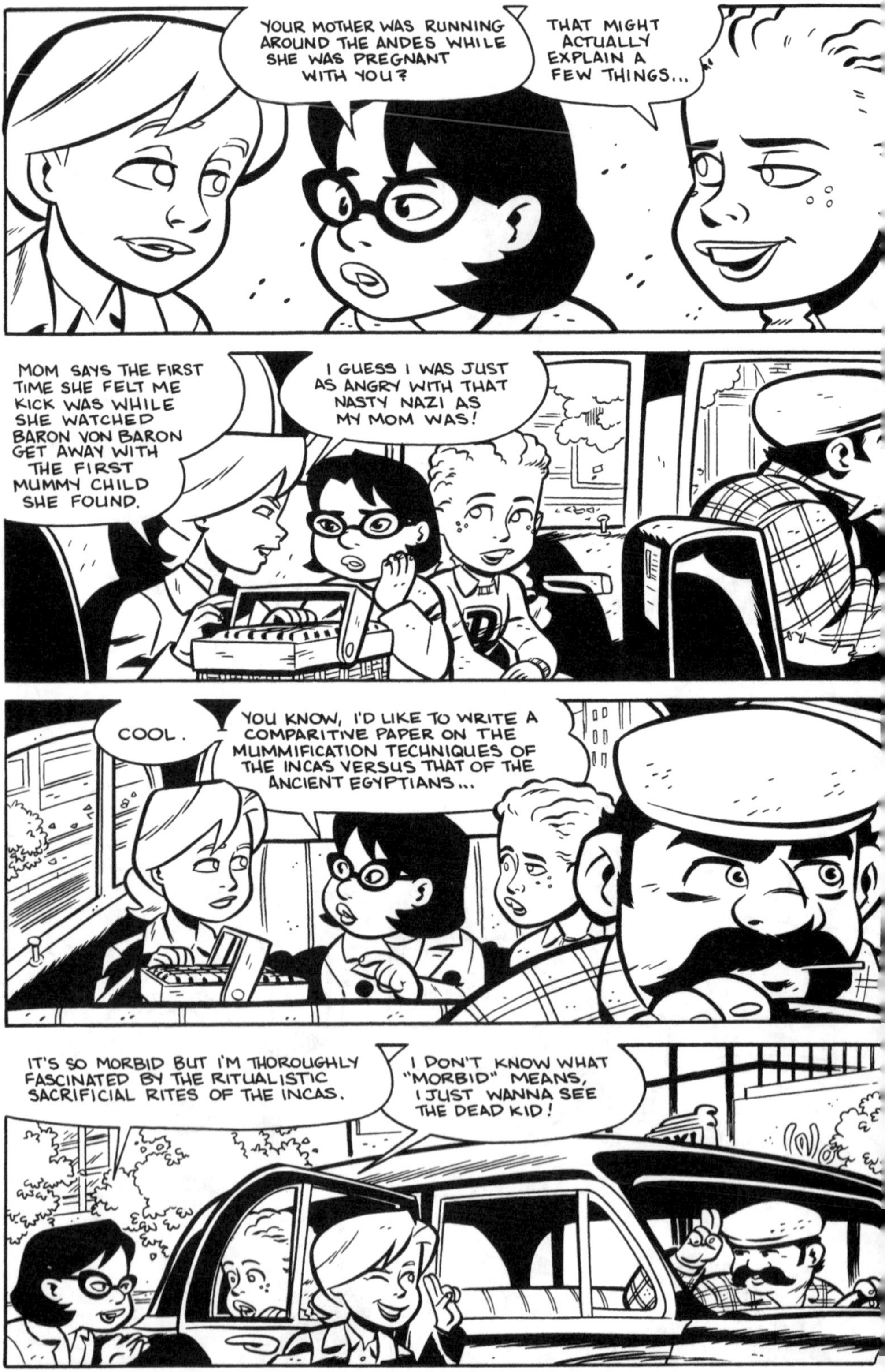
YOUR MOTHER WAS RUNNING AROUND THE ANDES WHILE SHE WAS PREGNANT WITH YOU?
THAT MIGHT ACTUALLY EXPLAIN A FEW THINGS...
MOM SAYS THE FIRST TIME SHE FELT ME KICK WAS WHILE SHE WATCHED BARON VON BARON GET AWAY WITH THE FIRST MUMMY CHILD SHE FOUND.
I GUESS I WAS JUST AS ANGRY WITH THAT NASTY NAZI AS MY MOM WAS!
COOL.
YOU KNOW, I'D LIKE TO WRITE A COMPARITIVE PAPER ON THE MUMMIFICATION TECHNIQUES OF THE INCAS VERSUS THAT OF THE ANCIENT EGYPTIANS...
IT'S SO MORBID BUT I'M THOROUGHLY FASCINATED BY THE RITUALISTIC SACRIFICIAL RITES OF THE INCAS.
I DON'T KNOW WHAT "MORBID" MEANS, I JUST WANNA SEE THE DEAD KID!

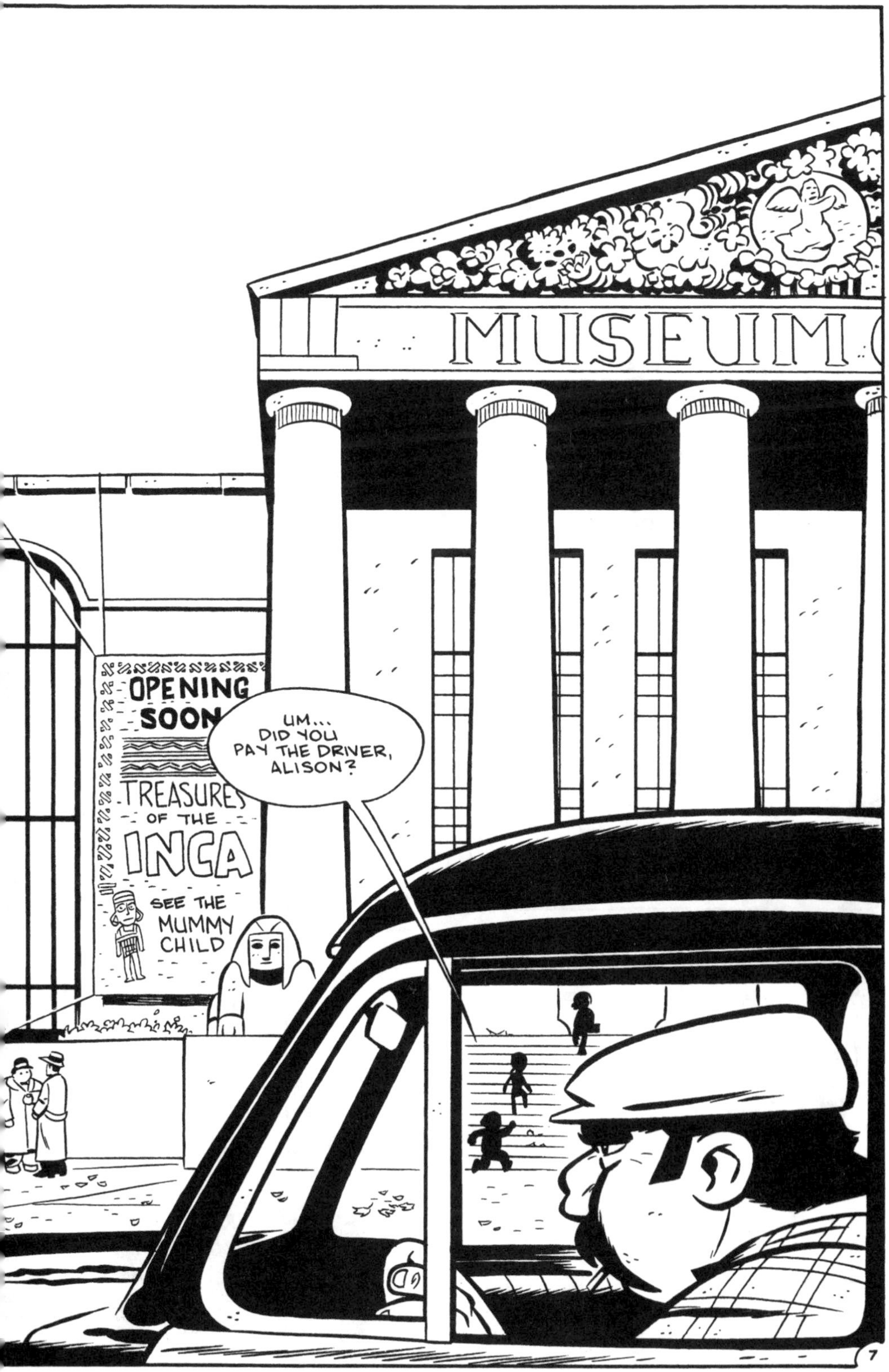
MUSEUM
OPENING SOON
TREASURES OF THE INCA
SEE THE MUMMY CHILD
UM... DID YOU PAY THE DRIVER, ALISON?

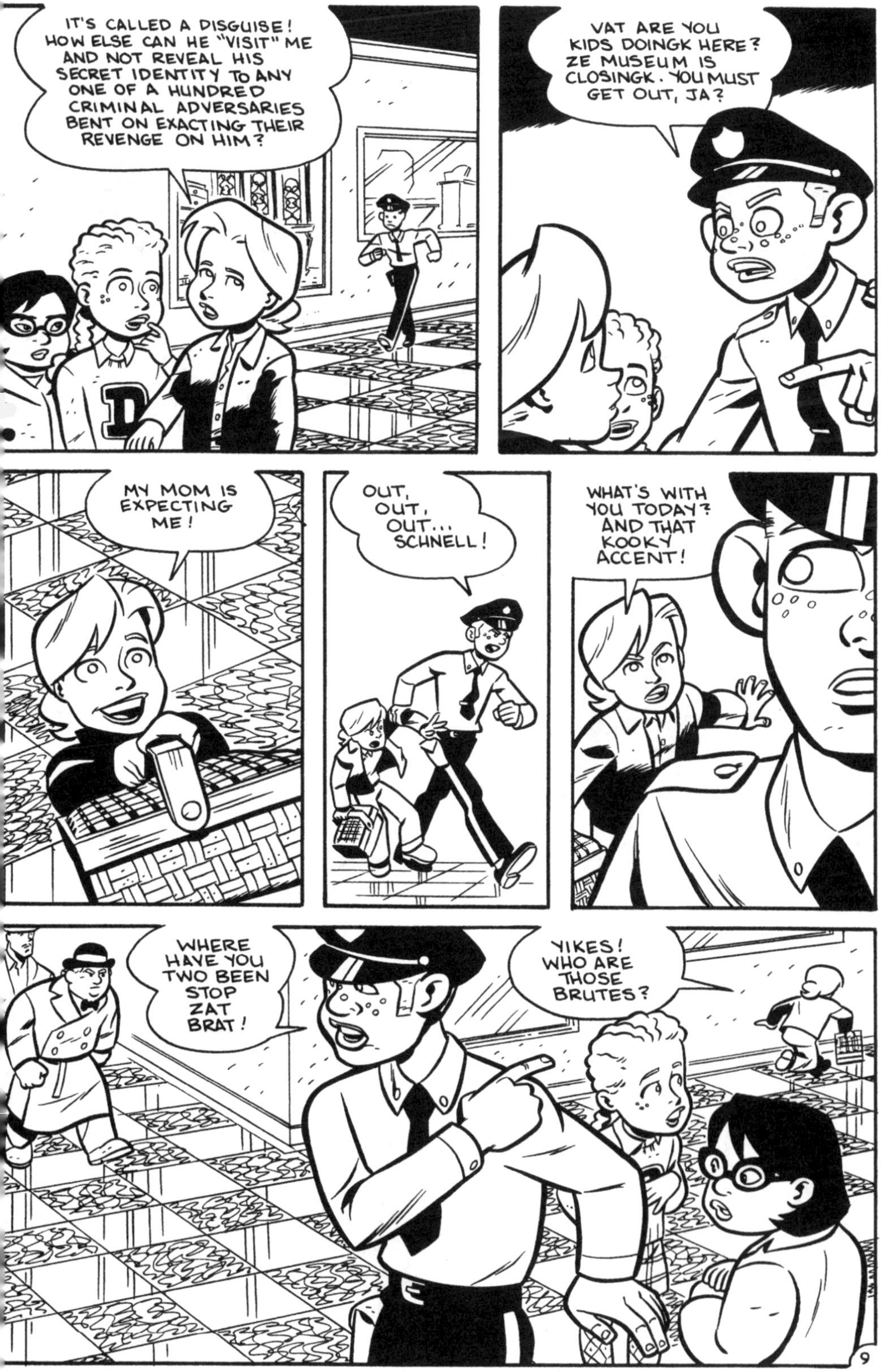
IT'S CALLED A DISGUISE! HOW ELSE CAN HE "VISIT" ME AND NOT REVEAL HIS SECRET IDENTITY TO ANY ONE OF A HUNDRED CRIMINAL ADVERSARIES BENT ON EXACTING THEIR REVENGE ON HIM?
VAT ARE YOU KIDS DOINGK HERE? ZE MUSEUM IS CLOSINGK. YOU MUST GET OUT, JA?
MY MOM IS EXPECTING ME!
OUT, OUT, OUT... SCHNELL!
WHAT'S WITH YOU TODAY? AND THAT KOOKY ACCENT!
WHERE HAVE YOU TWO BEEN STOP ZAT BRAT!
YIKES! WHO ARE THOSE BRUTES?

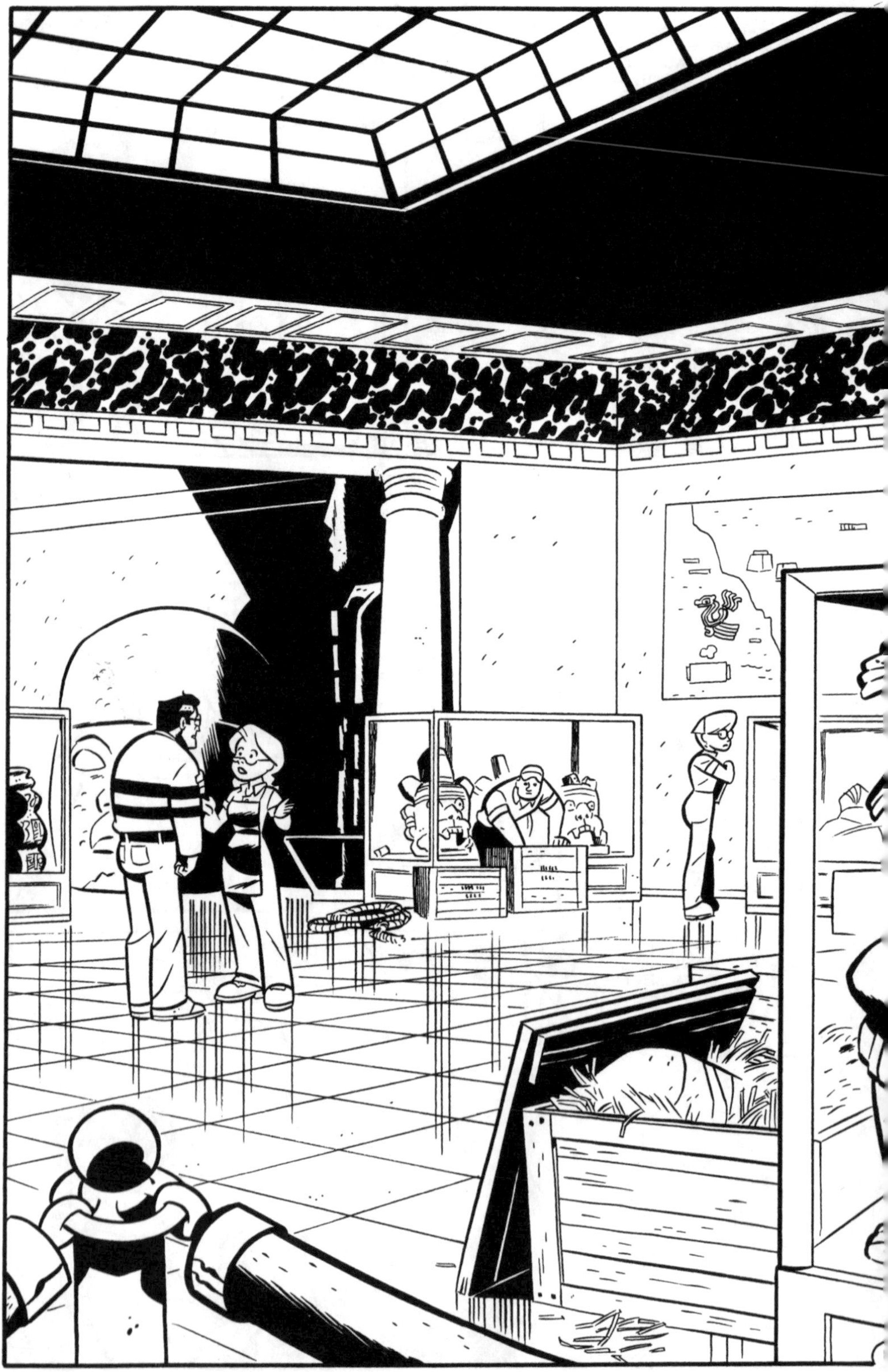

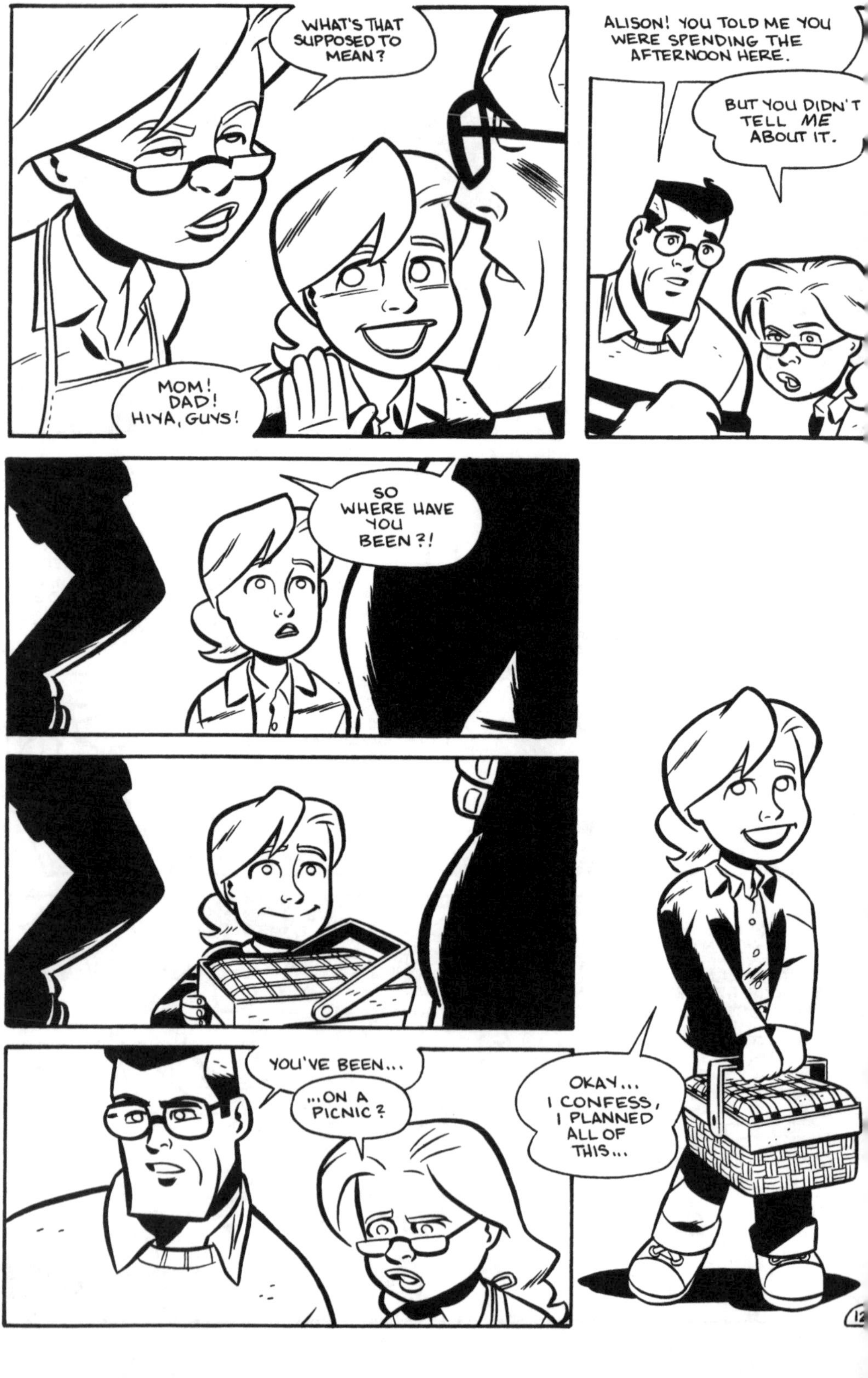
WHAT'S THAT SUPPOSED TO MEAN?
MOM! DAD! HIYA, GUYS!
ALISON! YOU TOLD ME YOU WERE SPENDING THE AFTERNOON HERE.
BUT YOU DIDN'T TELL *ME* ABOUT IT.
SO WHERE HAVE YOU BEEN?!
YOU'VE BEEN...
...ON A PICNIC?
OKAY... I CONFESS, I PLANNED ALL OF THIS...

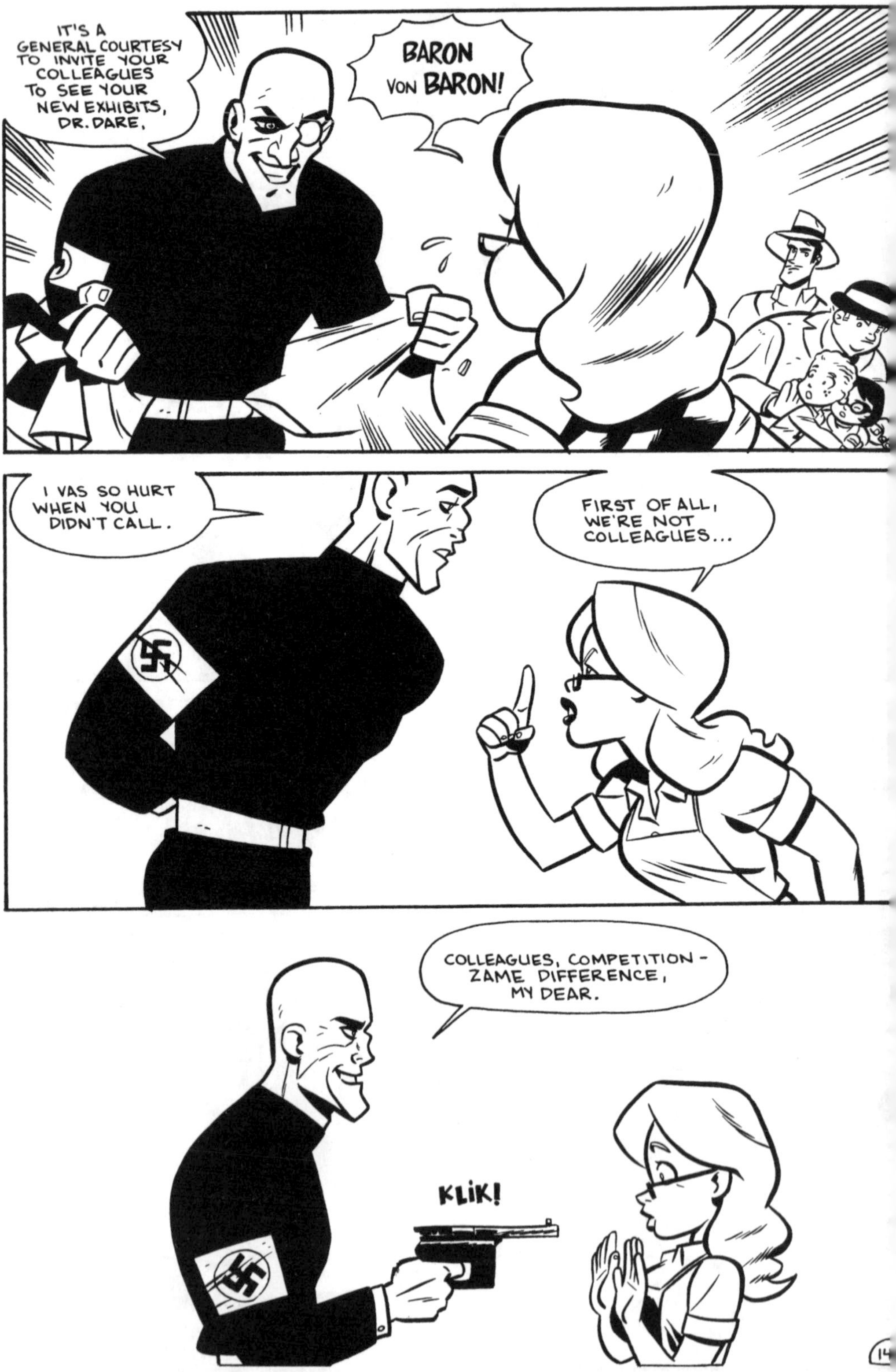
IT'S A GENERAL COURTESY TO INVITE YOUR COLLEAGUES TO SEE YOUR NEW EXHIBITS, DR. DARE.
BARON VON BARON!
I VAS SO HURT WHEN YOU DIDN'T CALL.
FIRST OF ALL, WE'RE NOT COLLEAGUES...
COLLEAGUES, COMPETITION - ZAME DIFFERENCE, MY DEAR.
KLIK!

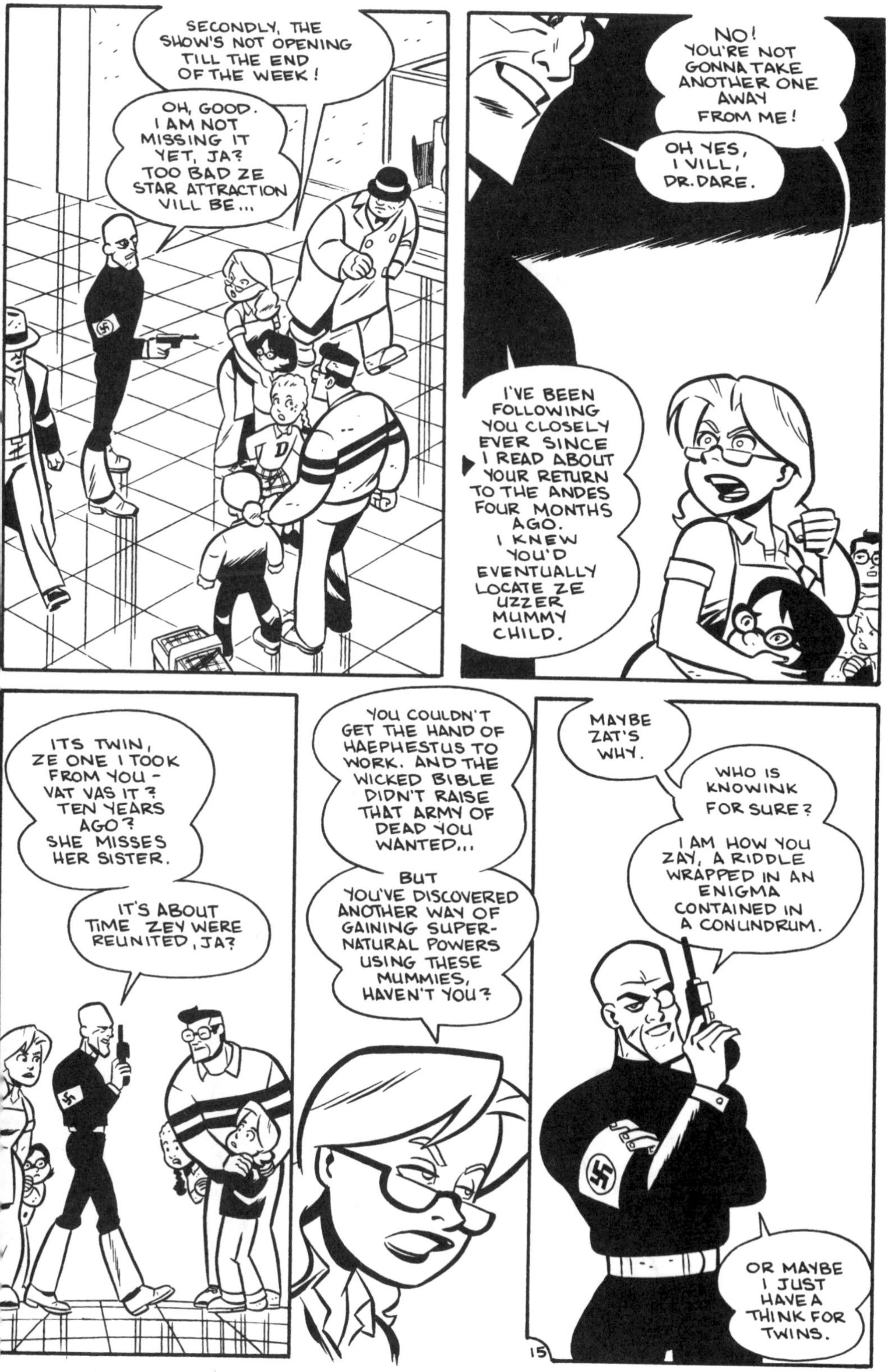
SECONDLY, THE SHOW'S NOT OPENING TILL THE END OF THE WEEK!
OH, GOOD. I AM NOT MISSING IT YET, JA? TOO BAD ZE STAR ATTRACTION VILL BE...
NO! YOU'RE NOT GONNA TAKE ANOTHER ONE AWAY FROM ME!
OH YES, I VILL, DR. DARE.
I'VE BEEN FOLLOWING YOU CLOSELY EVER SINCE I READ ABOUT YOUR RETURN TO THE ANDES FOUR MONTHS AGO. I KNEW YOU'D EVENTUALLY LOCATE ZE UZZER MUMMY CHILD.
ITS TWIN, ZE ONE I TOOK FROM YOU - VAT VAS IT? TEN YEARS AGO? SHE MISSES HER SISTER.
IT'S ABOUT TIME ZEY WERE REUNITED, JA?
YOU COULDN'T GET THE HAND OF HAEPHESTUS TO WORK. AND THE WICKED BIBLE DIDN'T RAISE THAT ARMY OF DEAD YOU WANTED...
BUT YOU'VE DISCOVERED ANOTHER WAY OF GAINING SUPER-NATURAL POWERS USING THESE MUMMIES, HAVEN'T YOU?
MAYBE ZAT'S WHY.
WHO IS KNOWINK FOR SURE?
I AM HOW YOU ZAY, A RIDDLE WRAPPED IN AN ENIGMA CONTAINED IN A CONUNDRUM.
OR MAYBE I JUST HAVE A THINK FOR TWINS.

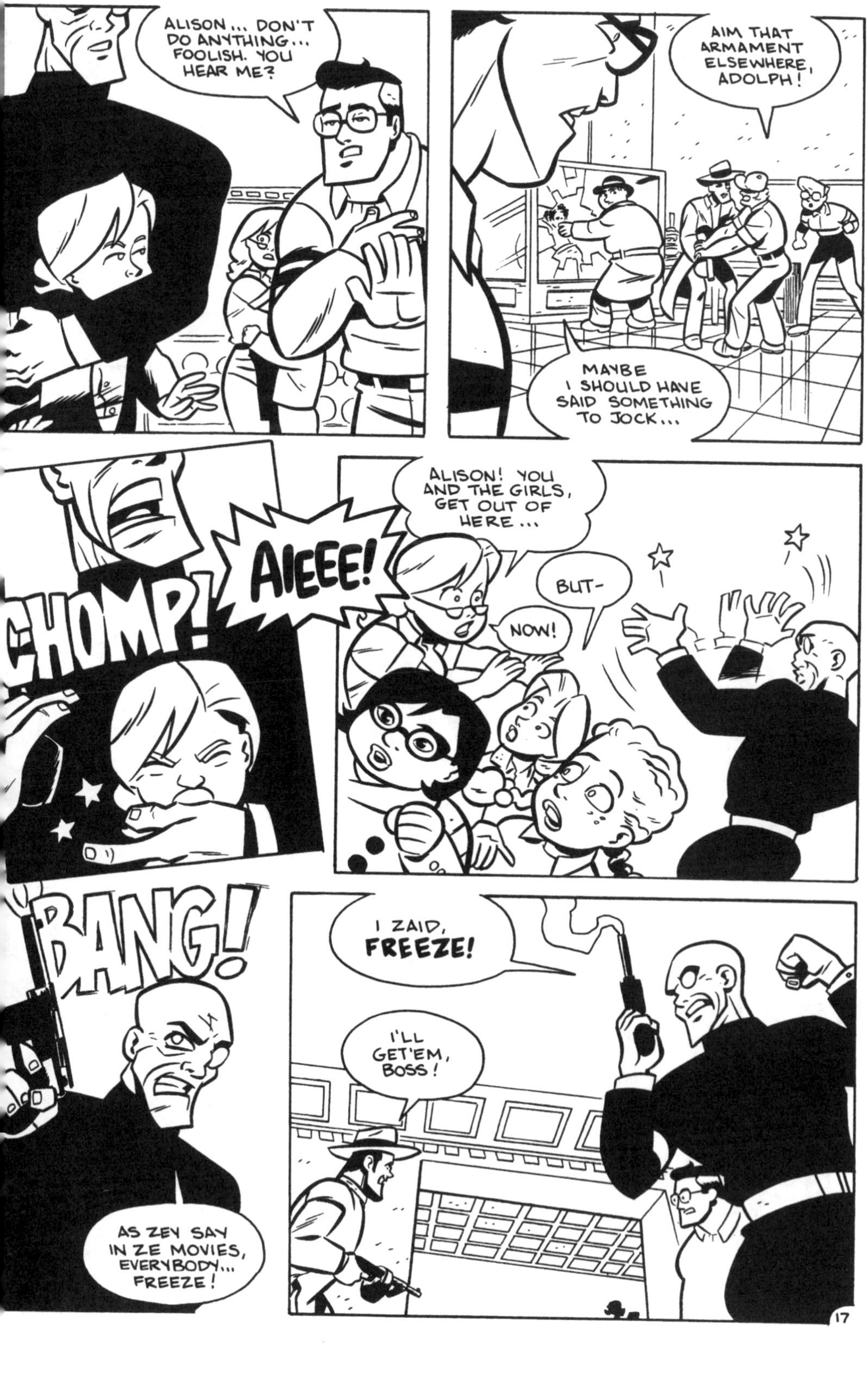
ALISON... DON'T DO ANYTHING... FOOLISH. YOU HEAR ME?
AIM THAT ARMAMENT ELSEWHERE, ADOLPH!
MAYBE I SHOULD HAVE SAID SOMETHING TO JOCK...
CHOMP!
AIEEE!
ALISON! YOU AND THE GIRLS, GET OUT OF HERE...
BUT-
NOW!
BANG!
AS ZEY SAY IN ZE MOVIES, EVERYBODY... FREEZE!
I ZAID, FREEZE!
I'LL GET'EM, BOSS!

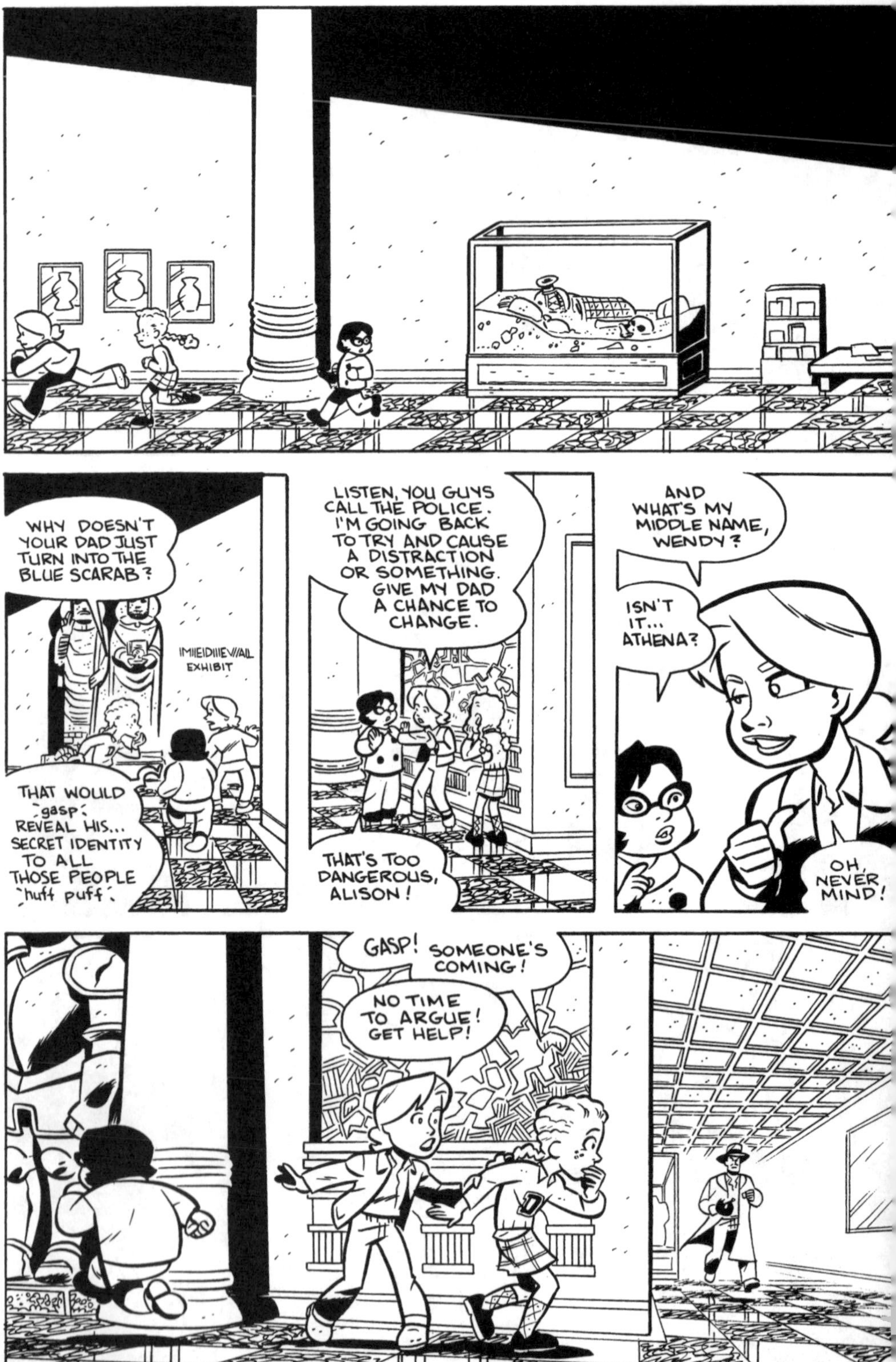
WHY DOESN'T YOUR DAD JUST TURN INTO THE BLUE SCARAB?
MEDIEVAL EXHIBIT
THAT WOULD ~gasp~ REVEAL HIS... SECRET IDENTITY TO ALL THOSE PEOPLE ~huff puff~
LISTEN, YOU GUYS CALL THE POLICE. I'M GOING BACK TO TRY AND CAUSE A DISTRACTION OR SOMETHING. GIVE MY DAD A CHANCE TO CHANGE.
THAT'S TOO DANGEROUS, ALISON!
AND WHAT'S MY MIDDLE NAME, WENDY?
ISN'T IT... ATHENA?
OH, NEVER MIND!
GASP! SOMEONE'S COMING!
NO TIME TO ARGUE! GET HELP!

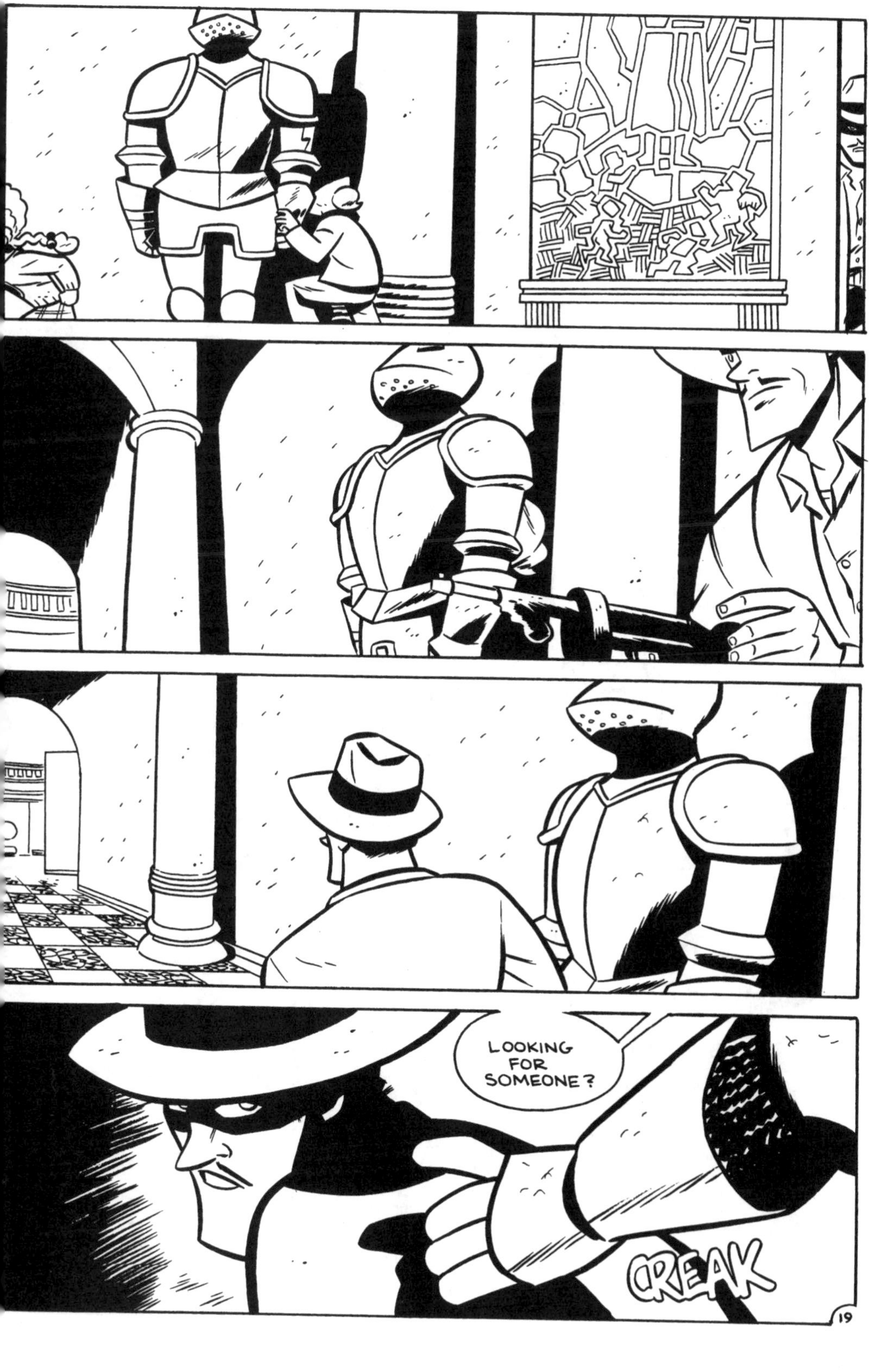
LOOKING FOR SOMEONE?
CREAK

23

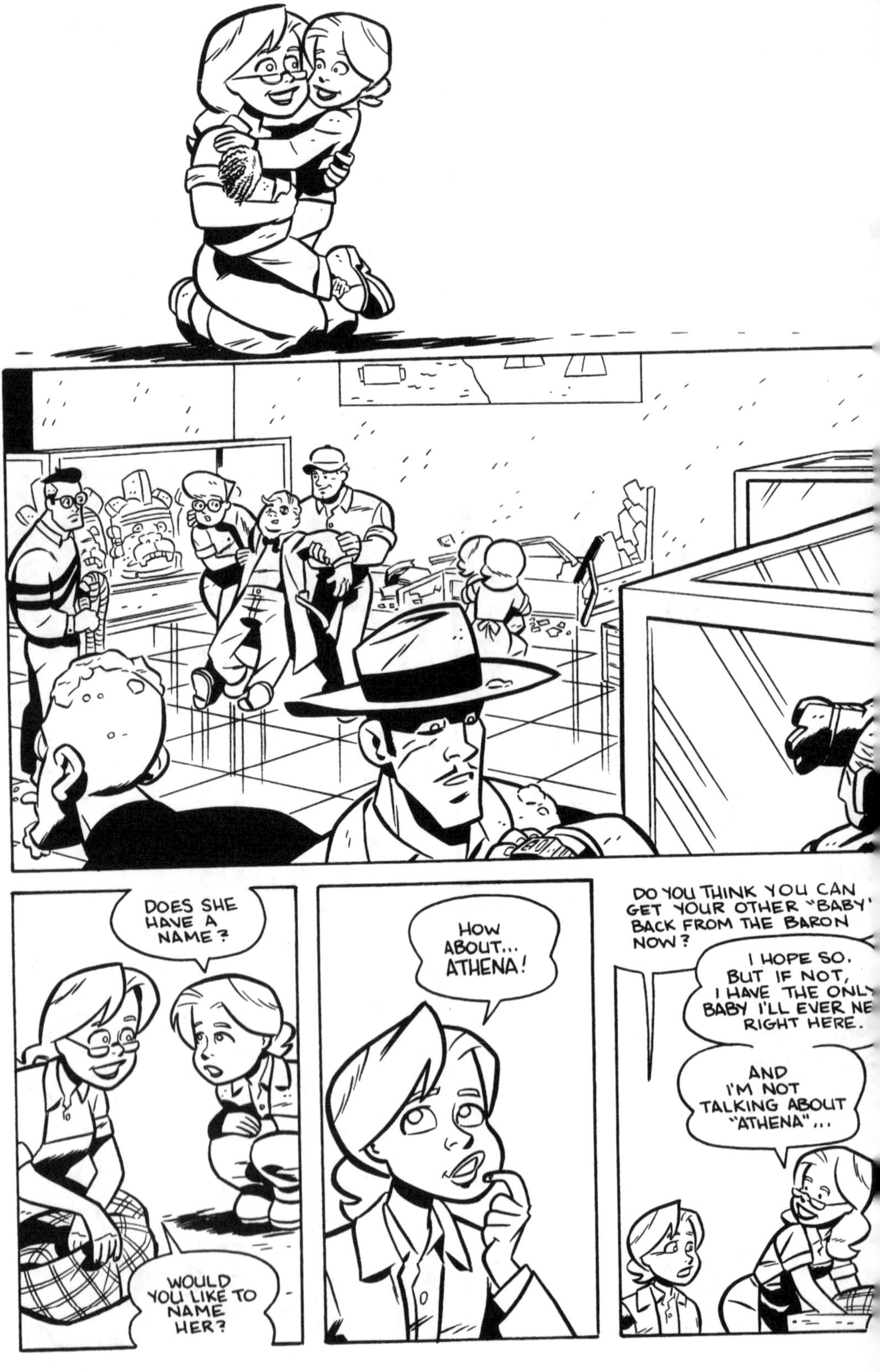
DOES SHE HAVE A NAME?
WOULD YOU LIKE TO NAME HER?
HOW ABOUT... ATHENA!
DO YOU THINK YOU CAN GET YOUR OTHER "BABY" BACK FROM THE BARON NOW?
I HOPE SO. BUT IF NOT, I HAVE THE ONLY BABY I'LL EVER NE RIGHT HERE.
AND I'M NOT TALKING ABOUT "ATHENA"...

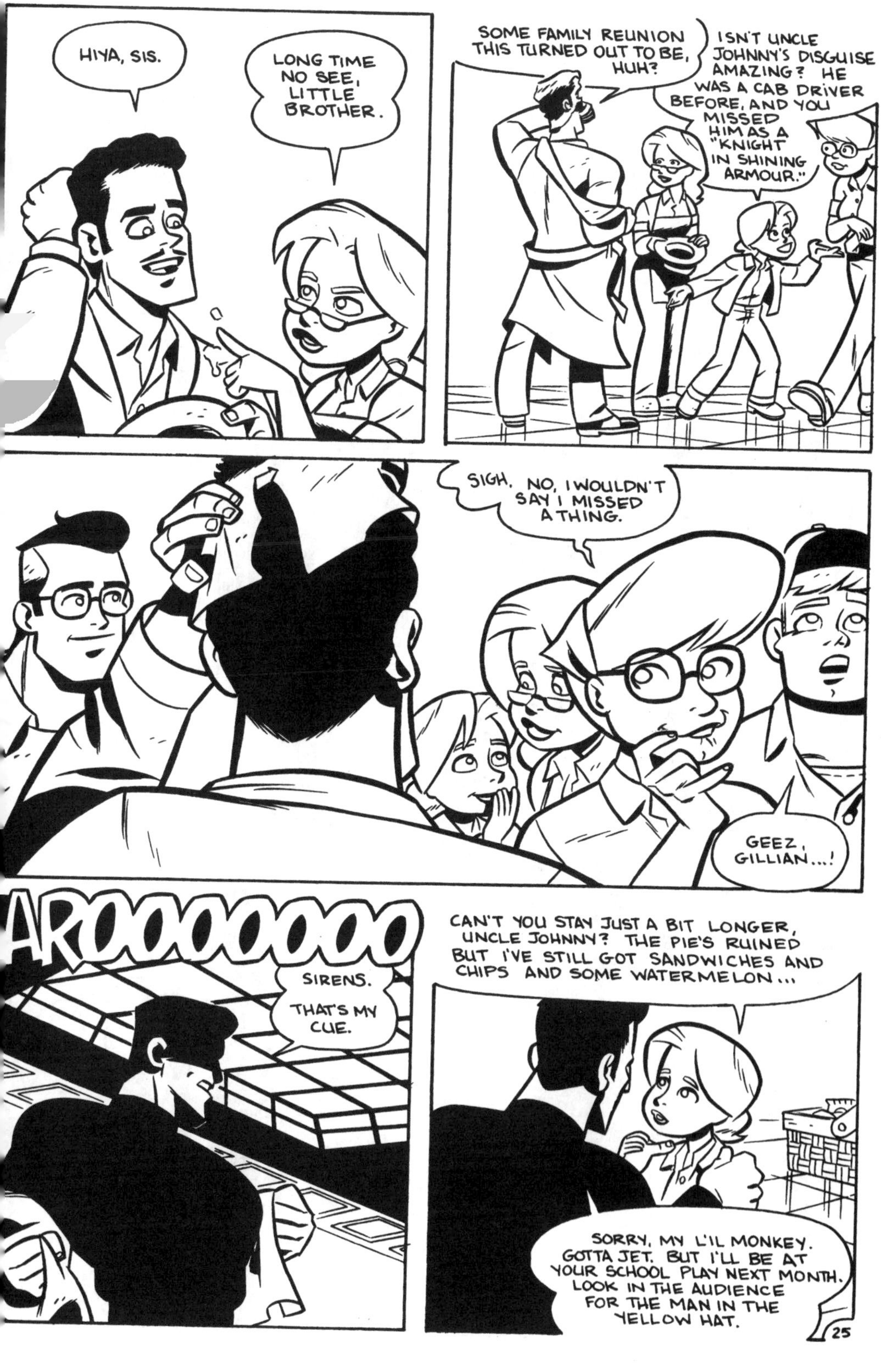
HIYA, SIS.
LONG TIME NO SEE, LITTLE BROTHER.
SOME FAMILY REUNION THIS TURNED OUT TO BE, HUH?
ISN'T UNCLE JOHNNY'S DISGUISE AMAZING? HE WAS A CAB DRIVER BEFORE, AND YOU MISSED HIM AS A "KNIGHT IN SHINING ARMOUR."
SIGH. NO, I WOULDN'T SAY I MISSED A THING.
GEEZ, GILLIAN...!
AROOOOOOOO
SIRENS.
THAT'S MY CUE.
CAN'T YOU STAY JUST A BIT LONGER, UNCLE JOHNNY? THE PIE'S RUINED BUT I'VE STILL GOT SANDWICHES AND CHIPS AND SOME WATERMELON...
SORRY, MY L'IL MONKEY. GOTTA JET. BUT I'LL BE AT YOUR SCHOOL PLAY NEXT MONTH. LOOK IN THE AUDIENCE FOR THE MAN IN THE YELLOW HAT.

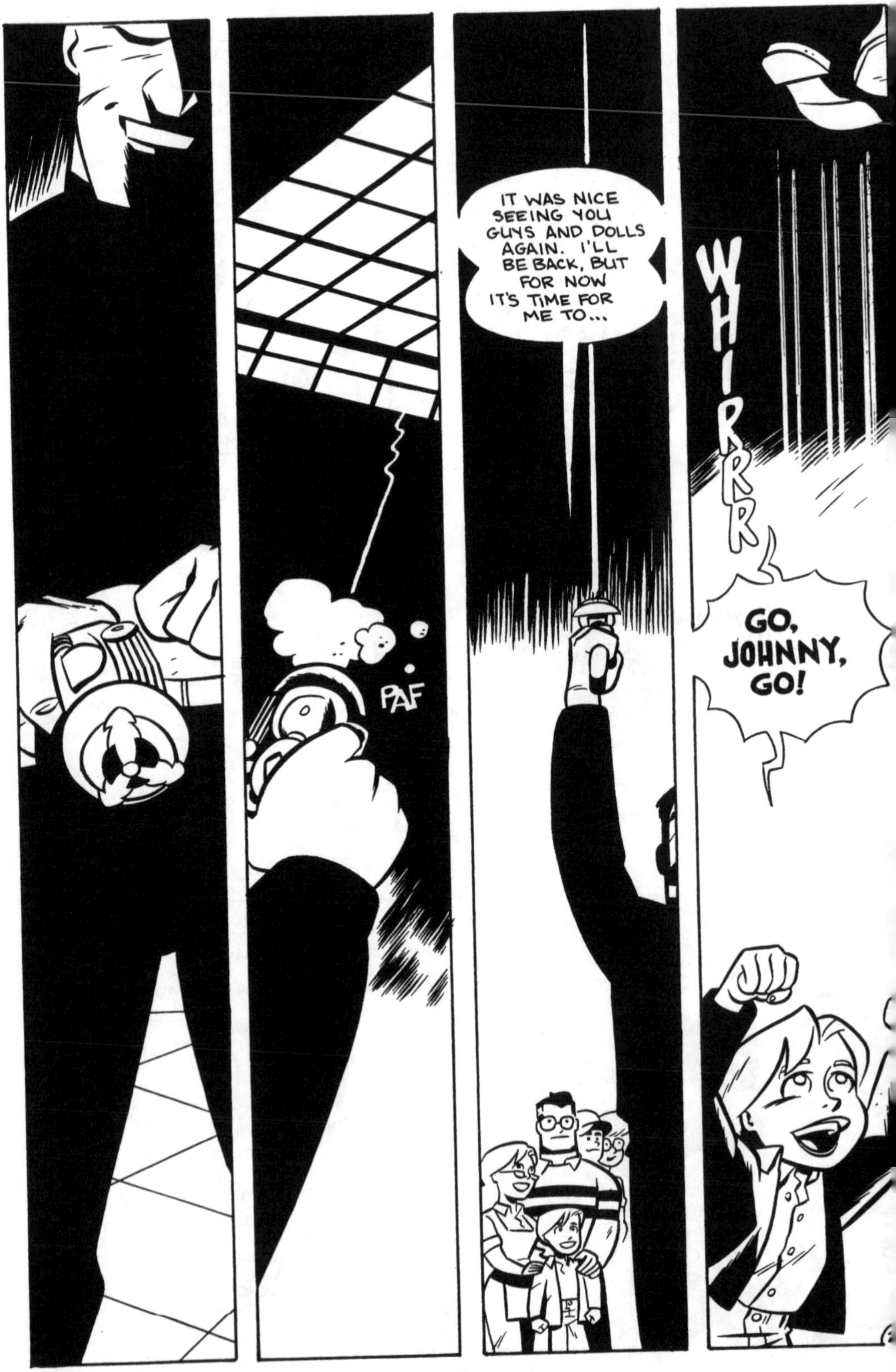
PAF
IT WAS NICE SEEING YOU GUYS AND DOLLS AGAIN. I'LL BE BACK, BUT FOR NOW IT'S TIME FOR ME TO...
WHIRRR
GO, JOHNNY, GO!

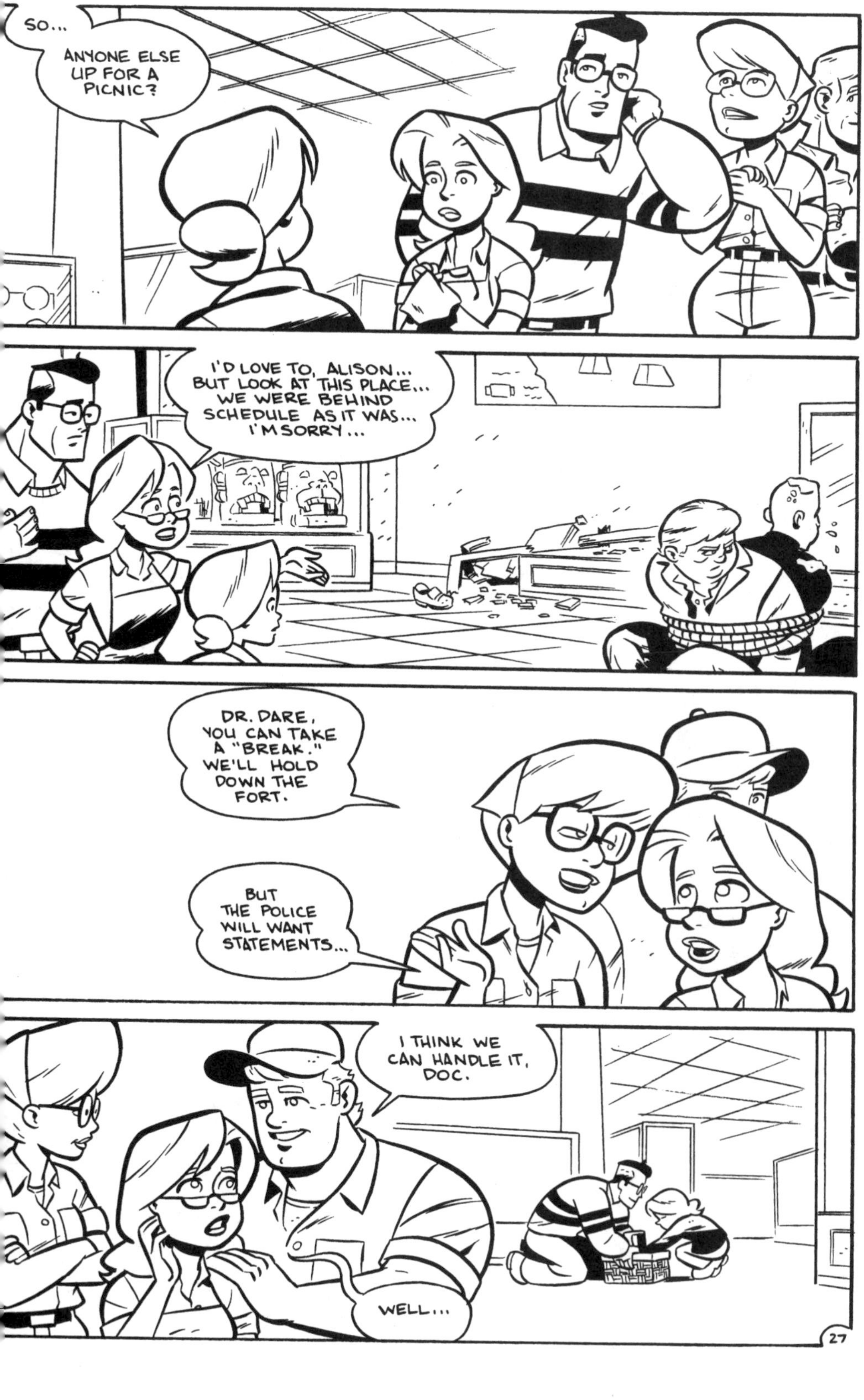
SO...
ANYONE ELSE UP FOR A PICNIC?
I'D LOVE TO, ALISON... BUT LOOK AT THIS PLACE... WE WERE BEHIND SCHEDULE AS IT WAS... I'M SORRY...
DR. DARE, YOU CAN TAKE A "BREAK." WE'LL HOLD DOWN THE FORT.
BUT THE POLICE WILL WANT STATEMENTS...
I THINK WE CAN HANDLE IT, DOC.
WELL...

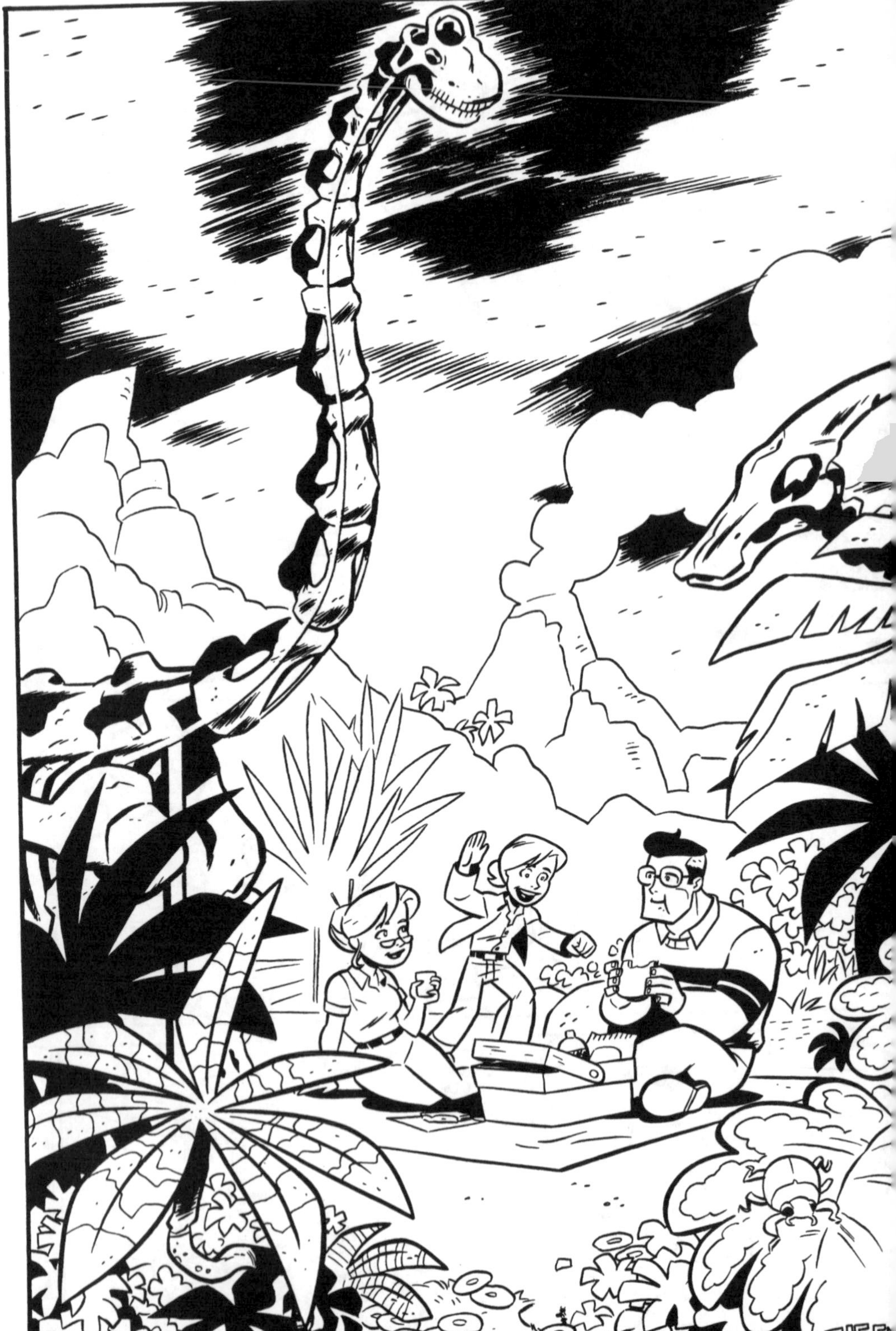
THE E

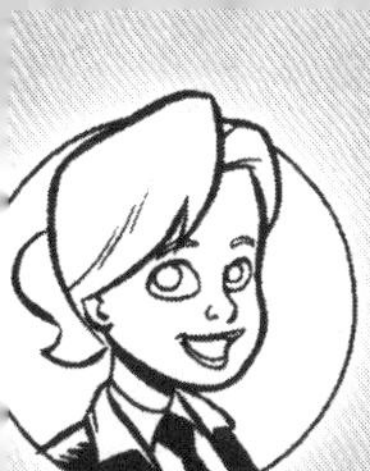

Alison's Daring Activity Sheet!

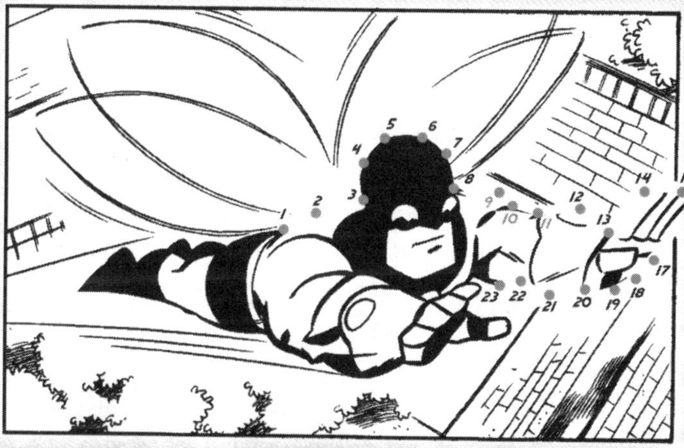
1
2
3
4
5
6
7
8
9
10
11
12
13
14
15
16
17
18
19
20
21
22
23

Help Alison's dad, the Blue Scarab, fly right by connecting the dots.

elp Alison finish her joke by decoding the hieroglyphs!

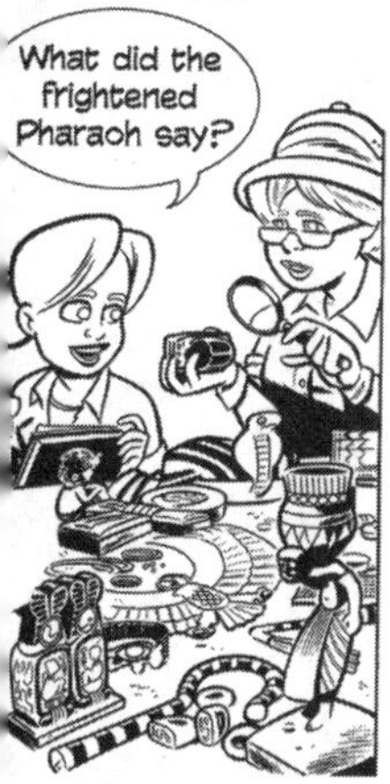
What did the frightened Pharaoh say?

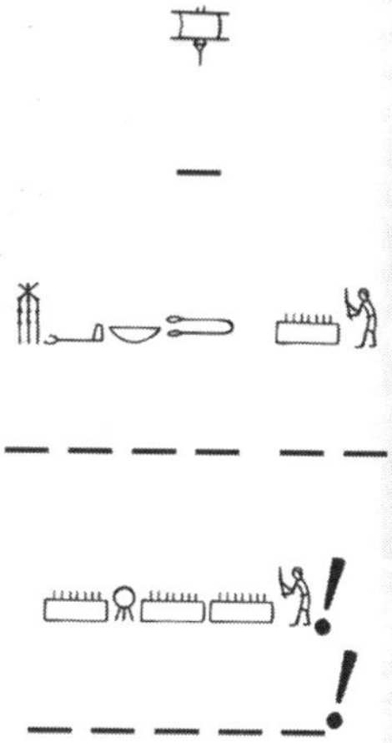

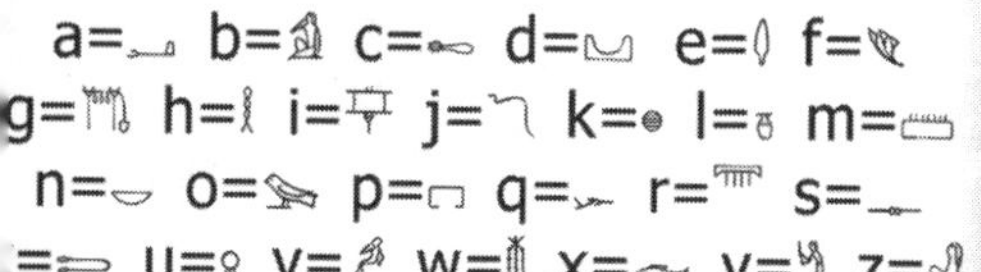
a=
b=
c=
d=
e=
f=
g=
h=
i=
j=
k=
l=
m=
n=
o=
p=
q=
r=
s=
=
u=
v=
w=
x=
y=
z=

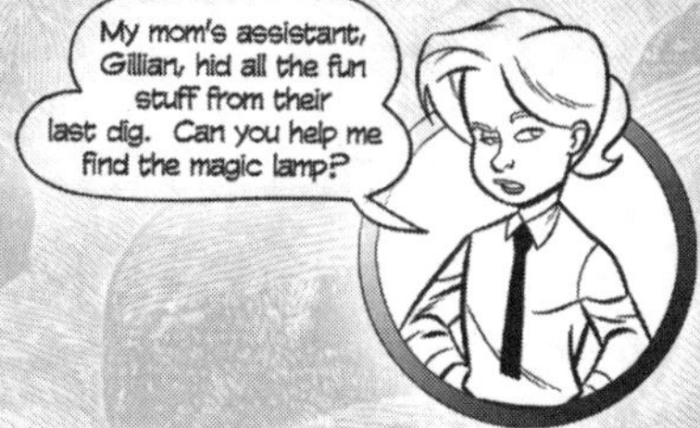
My mom's assistant, Gillian, hid all the fun stuff from their last dig. Can you help me find the magic lamp?

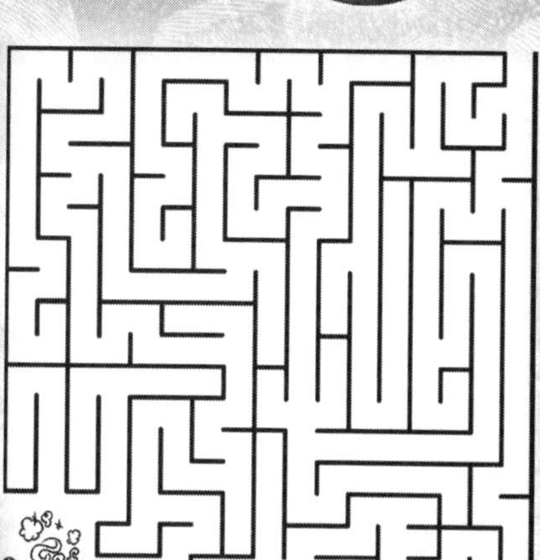

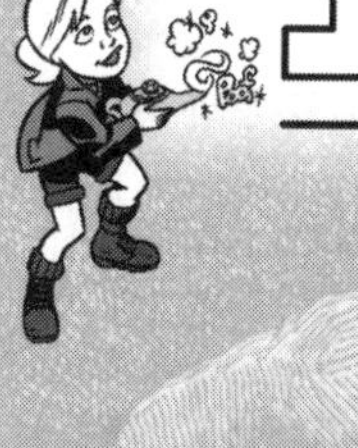
Poof